READER'S DIGEST

Fast & Fabulous

Home Accessories

READER'S DIGEST

Fast & Fabulous

Home Accessories

By the editors of *Handcraft Illustrated* magazine

The Reader's Digest Association, Inc.
Pleasantville, New York/Montreal

A Reader's Digest Book

Conceived and edited by the editors of *Handcraft Illustrated*
Designed by Amy Klee

The acknowledgments that appear on page 124 and the credits that appear
on page 125 are hereby made a part of this copyright page.

Library of Congress Cataloging in Publication Data
Home accessories/ by the editors of Handcraft illustrated.
        p.   cm. — (Fast and fabulous)
  Includes index.
  ISBN 0-7621-0027-3
  1. Handicraft. 2. House furnishings. 3. Interior decoration
accessories. I. Handcraft illustrated. II. Series.
TT157.H555   1998   97-31726
745.5—dc 21

Printed in the United States of America

A Note from the Editor

Decorative accessories are the small items or touches in a room that make us feel at home. A few pillows, a collection of framed photographs, or a cupboard for displaying small mementos are decorative accessories that can both pull a room together and revive your excitement about being there.

These accessories can also be considered small works of art. Whether bold or understated, they allow us to view a familiar space in a new way, and add a new level of comfort to our homes.

In this book, I have assembled an array of unique and easy-to-make designs that will add color and beauty to your home. You can make all of the items in this collection by hand, whether you have experience with a particular craft technique or not. As you move through the pages of this book, it is my hope that you will be inspired to make the kind of special objects that help you connect to your own home, and at the same time, enjoy the special pleasure that crafting brings.

Chapter One, for instance, includes containers of every description. You can work with decoupage, where fine illustrations are cut out and adhered to a tin cachepot; bright colors of acrylic paint, in order to add a festive plaid effect to a planter; or etching cream, an easy and forgiving medium that lets you add permanent graphic designs to the surface of glass.

In Chapter Two, you'll learn how to add mood and style to your rooms using handmade lighting fixtures. The natural beauty of fall leaves is captured in the glow of a laminated lampshade, made by sandwiching leaves between sheets of paper. Or transform a single seashell into a delicate candle.

Chapter Three contains a collection of frames made from easily found materials. You can cover a frame with vintage wallpaper, dried rose petals, or handmade paper, or create an antique look with a commercial patinating solution.

In Chapter Four, you'll see a variety of special effects for furniture. The projects include a farm table weathered with a simple paint and varnish technique, a striped cupboard made using a foolproof method based on strips of masking tape, and a handsome ottoman assembled from fabric, foam, and wood.

Rounding out the book, Chapter Five includes an assortment of unique accents, including miniature hinged fruit boxes, a paneled privacy screen for a cluttered desk, and a hanging sign that announces your love of home.

Remember that creativity is invited and expected. If you are a beginner, use these designs as surefire means of adding beauty to your home; if you are an intermediate or advanced crafter, use the items as jumping off points for your own designs and color choices. In either case, I hope you will use this collection to add energy and warmth to your life and your living spaces, to create a home overflowing with handmade projects of quality, style, and fine craftsmanship, and to experience the simple yet satisfying enjoyment we all feel from making something ourselves.

Carol Endler Sterbenz
Editor, Handcraft Illustrated

Contents

Lighting

Frames

Furniture

Decorative Items

Appendix

containers

French Tinware Cachepot

This elegant cachepot, which resembles an antique French planter, is created using two simple techniques. To give the cachepot its soft, ragged finish, start by basecoating the planter with chrome yellow paint. Next, combine burnt umber oil paint and clear polyurethane varnish to make a glaze, apply the glaze to the cachepot, then dab off some of the glaze to create a mottled look. The center oval cartouche is made with transfer medium, which, as the name implies, transfers a black-and-white or color image to a decal material. The image is then attached to the cachepot's painted surface and sealed. The resulting cachepot can be used as a planter, with a plastic liner inside, or as a decorative container on a sideboard or mantel.

———

You can decorate just about any type of tinware, except trays, using a cartouche made with transfer medium. This is because transferred images may not hold up to the abrasion of objects placed on the tray.

MATERIALS

■ Tinware container
■ Chrome yellow glossy enamel spray paint
■ Black semigloss quick-drying enamel paint
■ Forest green semigloss quick-drying enamel paint
■ Ivory gloss-finish quick-drying spray paint
■ Transfer medium
■ 2tbsp (29.6ml) satin-finish, quick-drying polyurethane varnish
■ 2oz (59.2ml) tube burnt umber artist's oil paint
■ 1oz (29.6ml) jar or tube pale gold oil paint
■ Spray-on metal primer (such as Krylon)

YOU'LL ALSO NEED:

2 photocopies of oval-shaped cartouche; flat, waterproof work surface such as laminated countertop or smooth, plastic cutting board; 1in (2.5cm) wide disposable paintbrush; #10 round brush; ¼in (6.4mm) round, stiff-bristled brush; scissors; rubber cement; small bowl; 2 disposable plastic containers; 1in (2.5cm) wide, low-tack painter's tape; kitchen sponge; soft cloth; paper towels; white distilled vinegar; paint thinner; 1in (2.5cm) wide masking tape; newspaper; tablespoon; protective eyewear for spray-painting steps; 4 small pieces of scrap wood; ruler; and plastic disposable gloves.

OTHER ITEMS, IF NECESSARY:

Cotton swabs (for removing paint smudges).

Instructions
Preparing the Tinware

1. Clean tinware. To clean container and remove oily residue, make 50-50 solution of vinegar and water. Rub entire container with soft cloth dipped in solution, then dry container thoroughly.

2. Apply primer to tinware. Cover workspace with newspaper, keep area well ventilated, and put on protective eyewear. Cover container's feet (or other brass parts) with masking tape. Tip container at an angle, mouth facing you, and spray-paint interior with primer. Let paint dry following manufacturer's recommendations, then apply second coat. To prevent rim of container from sticking to newspaper, turn it upside down and rest each corner on scrap wood. Apply one coat primer to outside and bottom of container. Let dry following manufacturer's recommendations, then apply second coat. Let dry thoroughly.

3. Apply basecoat to tinware. Spray-paint outside and bottom of container with chrome yellow paint. Let dry following manufacturer's recommendations, then apply second coat. If necessary, apply third coat to cover thin spots. Stand container upright on feet and let dry thoroughly.

4. Paint interior finish. Using ¼in (6.4mm) round brush, tablespoon, and one plastic container, mix one part forest green paint with four parts black paint. Using disposable paintbrush, apply even, thin coat of paint to tinware container's interior. Check seams and corners for excess or pooling paint; if necessary, remove with paintbrush. Set container aside to dry between 4 and 8 hours or follow manufacturer's recommendations. Clean tablespoon, round brush, and work surfaces with paint thinner.

Preparing the Cartouche

A. Tape the image down, then brush on six coats of transfer medium.

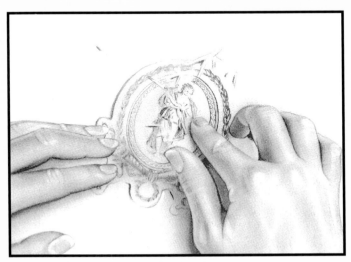

B. Soak the image in warm water, then rub the back gently to roll off the paper.

Making the Cachepot

1. Transfer image. Attach one photocopy of cartouche to waterproof surface by taping it around edges with masking tape. Apply six successive coats of transfer medium with #10 brush (see illustration A, at right), brushing on each coat perpendicular to preceding one to minimize brush marks. Let each coat dry 15 minutes before applying next coat. Paint over entire cartouche as well as ½ in (12.7mm) beyond outline. Wash out brush thoroughly between coats. Let cartouche dry 24 hours.

For variation on this design, substitute any one of many copyright-free black and white images available from companies such as Dover Publications.

2. Prepare cartouche for adhering. Peel cartouche off surface and remove tape from edges. Clean surface with damp sponge and dry with paper towel. Soak cartouche in bowl of warm water 1 hour, then lay it face down on dry, clean surface. Rub back of cartouche gently with fingertip to roll off paper in small pieces (illustration B). Continue until all paper is removed and copied image is visible. Let cartouche dry on countertop 1 hour, or until almost transparent. If dry cartouche is not transparent, repeat soaking, rubbing, and drying processes.

3. Create stencil mask. Using scissors, carefully cut out oval center of second photocopied cartouche (illustration C), then discard cutout center. Trim edges of oval shape neatly. Lay image face down on clean piece of newspaper and apply thin coat rubber cement to 1in (2.5cm) wide swath around inside edges of cutout area. Let dry 5 minutes, then apply second coat. Let dry 15 minutes. Center stencil mask on one side of container (illustration D), then press in place with fingertips.

4. Paint ivory oval. Leave oval area inside image exposed, then cover remainder of container by taping on newspaper. Cover workspace with newspaper, keep area well ventilated, and put on protective eyewear. Lay container on side with exposed area facing up, then spray-paint oval with one to two thin, even coats ivory paint. Pull stencil mask away immediately to prevent ivory paint from bleeding under it. If paint bleeds, remove

smudges using cotton swab dipped in paint thinner. Let container dry at least 2 hours. When ivory paint is dry, remove any remaining rubber cement by rubbing with fingers.

5. Mix and apply glaze. To make glaze, combine polyurethane varnish and pea-sized dab of burnt umber paint in second plastic container, then mix thoroughly using ¼in (6.4mm) round brush. Pull on plastic gloves. Crumple one paper towel into loose ball and dip one side into glaze. Apply one thin, even coat of glaze on one side of tinware container by smearing over paint with light, circular motion. To create mottled effect, blot painted surface with clean paper towel to remove glaze. Repeat on each side of container, then let dry 2 hours. For side with ivory oval, finish by wiping glaze away from oval with paper towel dipped in paint thinner. Clean up using paint thinner.

6. Adhere cartouche. Trim edges of transparent image to within ⅛in (3.2mm) of image. Lay cartouche face down on clean work surface, then apply thin, even coat of transfer medium to back of image and container using #10 brush. Position cartouche on container, matching rounded edges with ivory oval, then smooth in place with fingers (illustration E). Press edges down firmly and force out any trapped bubbles. Remove excess transfer medium with moistened sponge. Last, apply final glazing coat of transfer medium to entire side of container. Let dry 30 minutes.

7. Add finishing details. Apply low-tack painter's tape under container's outside rolled rim, lining up edge of tape with underside of rolled rim. Apply tape around container's interior approximately ⅛in (3.2mm) from and parallel to rim. Using ¼in (6.4mm) round brush, paint exposed rim area with gold oil paint (illustration F). If desired, paint other details gold, such as ring handles, knobs, or feet. Let paint dry overnight. Clean any tools or surfaces using paint thinner. Remove tape from top edges, then remove tape from feet or other brass parts.

Making the Cachepot

C. Cut out the oval center of the second photocopied image.

D. Center the stencil mask on one side of the container.

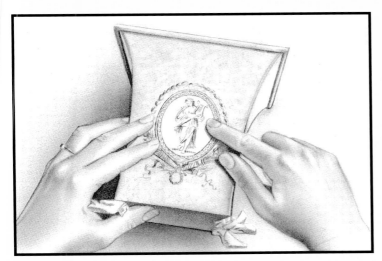

E. After adding the mottled finish, adhere the image inside the ivory oval.

F. Finish the cachepot by painting the rim with gold paint.

Arts and Crafts Bandbox

This decorative bandbox captures the style of the Arts and Crafts Movement in two ways: The box is covered with an Arts and Crafts–style wallpaper border, and the box's woven top has been treated to simulate the look of aged copper. The resulting piece is true to its 19th-century roots, but will fit in with just about any decorating style.

———

For truly authentic Arts and Crafts–style wallpaper, find an outlet for papers from Bradbury & Bradbury, of Benicia, California. This company still hand-prints several original wallpaper designs of William Morris, a noted Arts and Crafts designer.

MATERIALS

- 5in (12.7cm) high x 8in (20.3cm) diameter round chipboard box with woven lid
- 7in (17.8cm) wide Arts–and–Crafts–style wallpaper border
- 2oz. (59.6ml) acrylic craft paint
- Copper solution
- Green patinating solution
- Wallpaper adhesive

YOU'LL ALSO NEED:

quilter's grid ruler; craft knife; self-healing cutting mat; 1in (2.5cm) and 2in (5.1cm) foam brushes; ½in (12.7mm) disposable bristle brush; ¼in (6.4mm) round brush and/or ½in (12.7mm) flat brush; scissors; pencil; paper towels; latex gloves; splash goggles; and newsprint.

Instructions

1. Create copper patina. Remove lid from box; set aside box. Protect work surface with several layers newsprint. Follow manufacturer's instructions and safety precautions for copper and patinating solutions. Wearing latex gloves and goggles, and using 1in (2.5cm) foam brush, apply two coats copper solution to woven section of box lid. Let dry 1 hour after each coat. Apply third coat copper solution, let dry until tacky (5-10 minutes), then use bristle brush to apply patinating solution over copper surface. Pale green patina will emerge within 10 to 25 minutes. If necessary after that time, apply additional coats to intensify verdigris effect. Let dry overnight.

2. Paint box. Using flat or round brush, paint rim that surrounds woven section to match one color in wallpaper background (see illustration A, at right). Paint box bottom, box interior, and lid interior. Let dry 1 hour.

3. Cut wallpaper border to fit box. Wrap wallpaper border once around box, overlap 5in (12.7cm), and cut with scissors. Fold overlap under until you achieve pleasing pattern transition at seam. Make tick mark on underlap ½in (12.7mm) from seam (illustration B). Using grid ruler and craft knife, cut strip at fold and at mark. Wrap strip around box, even at bottom edge, and mark strip ⅜in (9.5mm) above box rim. Using grid ruler and craft knife, trim strip lengthwise even with this mark (illustration C). Test-fit narrower strip around box lid, even at top edge; trim, if necessary, so strip extends no more than ½in (12.7mm) beyond lower rim.

4. Glue wallpaper strips to box. Lay strips face down on newsprint. Using 2in (5.1cm) foam brush, apply wallpaper adhesive to back of wider strip, brushing out beyond edges for full coverage. Let rest 3 to 5 minutes. Set side of box against middle of strip, matching lower edges (illustration D). Turn box upright. Working from middle out to edges, use paper towel to press strip smooth against box all around; overlap ends to make seam (illustration E). Using scissors, clip into top allowance every ½in (12.7mm), then press allowance over onto box rim all around (illustration F). Wipe off any oozing adhesive. Glue narrow strip to lid in same way, pressing allowance onto lower inside rim. Let box and lid dry overnight (illustration G).

Covering the Box

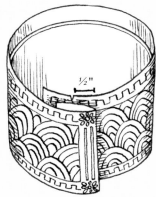

A. Apply the patina to the top of the lid, then paint the box.

B. Test-fit the wallpaper border around the box and determine a pleasing pattern overlap.

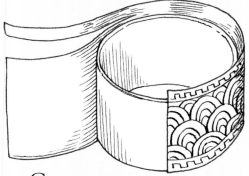

C. Trim off the excess paper and save it to cover the box lid.

D. Coat the wider strip with wallpaper adhesive, then set the box in the middle.

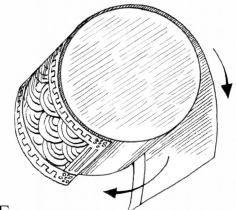

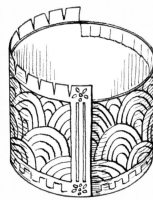

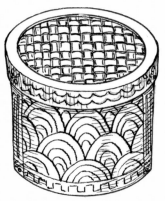

E. Turn the box upright and smooth the strip around it.

F. Clip and glue down the allowance on the box's top edge.

G. Glue the narrow strip around the lid, then let the lid and the box dry overnight.

21

Star Frost Vase

In the past, frosting glass was a craft better left to skilled experts. Today, however, it's possible to transform an ordinary glass vase into a frosted work of art using a safe and simple product called glass-etching cream. The cream is used in combination with ready-made star-shaped stencils, which are taped in place on the vase. Instead of using paint, however, to fill in the open area, you'll use glass-etching cream, which chemically reacts with the glass. When the frosting process is complete—anywhere from 1 to 4 minutes—the cream is removed under running water and the vase is left to dry, revealing the frosted design. This vase was created with larger stars near the middle of the vase, and graduated smaller stars on the top and bottom.

———

For a different look entirely, create a vase with frosted polka dots. Dip a brush in etching solution, then twirl the brush on the glassware to create the dots. Proceed as for the star frost vase, rinsing the cream away under running water.

MATERIALS

- **Glass vase**
- **Glass-etching cream and stencil kit**

YOU'LL ALSO NEED:

½in **(12.7mm) wide masking tape;** ½in **(12.7mm) wide disposable paintbrush; latex gloves; scissors; window-cleaning solution; rubbing alcohol; kraft paper; felt-tip marker; paper towels; and watch or clock.**

Instructions

1. Prepare vase for frosting. Clean vase with window cleaner and paper towel. Using felt-tip marker, mark 35 to 40 small dots on vase interior for positioning of stars. To change layout, remove felt-tip marks using paper towel and rubbing alcohol.

2. Cut and apply stencils. Cut stencil sheet along solid lines to separate into 35 to 40 individual squares. Handle sheet and squares by edges and avoid touching stencil's cloudy (adhesive) surface. Position 8 to 10 stencils on outside of vase in accordance with felt-tip pen dots marked in step 1. Position stencil adhesive side down, and fasten each in place along one edge with masking tape. Using flat edge of wooden stick provided in kit, rub shiny surface of each stencil until tone changes from dark to light blue (see illustration A,

right). When entire image has turned color, lift off clear backing, leaving blue star stencil adhered to surface (illustration B).

3. Mask stencils. To protect surrounding glass from etching cream, mask all four outside edges of each stencil with small pieces of masking tape (illustration C). To seal tape tightly, press down tape edges with wooden stick. Hold vase up to light and check each stencil for lifted edges, bubbles, pinholes, tears, or cracks. (Even tiny cracks will allow etching cream to seep beyond stencil and mar the effect.) Fix any of above problems with small pieces of tape.

4. Frost stencils. Work beside sink and provide ample ventilation. Cover work area with kraft paper and wear latex gloves. Turn vase upside down on kraft paper. Dip paintbrush into cream and dab ¹⁄₁₆in (1.6mm) thick coat on each star stencil, staying within taped areas (illustration D). Dab over any thin spots. Clean up any spatters or drips of cream immediately with damp paper towel. Allow cream to remain on glass from 1 to 4 minutes, then rinse off vase under warm running tap water (illustration E). Set vase aside and thoroughly rinse sink. Peel off stencils and tape from vase and remove any remaining residue using window cleaner and paper towels (illustration F). When glass is thoroughly dry, frosted stars will appear. Repeat appropriate parts of Steps 2 to 4 with remaining stars, working in groups of 8 to 10 until all stars are etched. When all stars are frosted, remove felt-tip pen marks from inside of vase using paper towels and rubbing alcohol. Clean paintbrush with warm water.

DESIGNER'S TIP

For variation on this design, consider using glass-etching cream to highlight relief areas on a bottle, spell someone's name on a mug, or add seasonal motifs to wine glasses.

Frosting the Vase

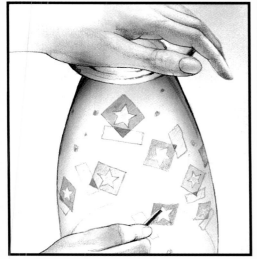

A. After positioning the stencils on the outside of the vase, rub the shiny surface of each stencil until the tone changes from dark to light blue.

B. When the entire image has become light blue, lift off the clear backing.

C. To protect the surrounding glass from the etching cream, mask all four edges of each stencil with small pieces of masking tape.

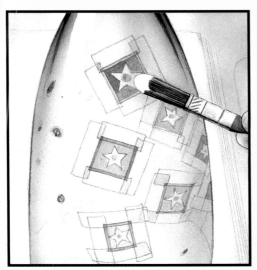

D. Apply a generous coat of etching cream to each star stencil, taking care to stay within the taped areas. Dab over any thin areas.

E. Allow the cream to remain on the glass for 1 to 4 minutes, then rinse it off by holding the vase under warm running tap water. Rinse the sink thoroughly.

F. Peel off the stencils and the tape from the vase and remove any remaining residue using window cleaner and paper towels. When dry, the frosted stars will appear.

Painted Plaid Cachepot

The beauty of this painted plaid cachepot revolves around contrast. The vibrant colors chosen to decorate this container not only complement and highlight each other but also offset the delicate wheatgrass inside. The loose plaid pattern uses stripes of periwinkle, red-orange, fuchsia, and foliage green acrylic paint on top of a canary yellow basecoat. For the whimsical finishing touches, you can add dots of paint along the rim and through the stripes, crisscrossing squiggly lines, and a gold border.

—

If you can't find the exact cachepot shown at left, which measures 6¼in (15.9cm) wide x 5¾in (14.6cm) high, look for a container with straight sides, which makes the continuation of the stripes from one side to the next quite simple. This is much trickier to do with a flared container.

MATERIALS

- 6¼in (15.9cm) square x 5¾in (14.6cm) high tin cachepot
- Canary yellow latex enamel paint
- 2oz (59.2ml) acrylic paints in the following colors: foliage green, fuchsia, periwinkle, red-orange, and white
- 2oz (59.2ml) pure pigment color: crimson
- 2oz (59.2ml) gold paint
- 2oz (59.2ml) pearlescent paint
- White sandable primer
- Clear spray shellac

YOU'LL ALSO NEED:

1in (2.5cm) wide painter's tape; 45° triangle; scissors; two ½in (12.7mm) wide flat sabeline brushes; #3 round sabeline brush; 3 fine-tipped plastic paint syringes; newsprint; white vinegar; 1-cup (0.24L) bowl; measuring cup; soft cloths; paint palette or moist paper towel; and cellulose sponge.

Instructions

1. Paint basecoat. To clean container and remove oily residue, make 50-50 solution of vinegar and water. Rub entire container with soft cloth dipped in solution, then dry container thoroughly. Using flat brush, coat container with primer follow-ing manufacturer's instructions. Let dry 1 hour. Mask ball feet with tape. Spray inside and outside of container with three to four very light coats latex enamel, letting dry 10 minutes between coats. Let container dry 24 hours. Remove tape from feet.

2. Mask container for left diagonal stripes. Set container on level surface. To mark 45° diagonal stripes, stand triangle on edge, flat against outer wall of container, with angle slanting toward upper left. Press painter's tape to surface along triangle edge (see illustration A, at right). Repeat to add second piece of tape, allowing random-width space between tape strips for painted stripe. Press on six additional diagonal tapes around container, taping around corners onto adjacent sides. To vary pattern, add more tape to make some masked areas wider (illustration B). Confirm angles with triangle.

3. Paint left diagonal stripes. Using ½in (12.7mm) flat brushes, apply periwinkle and red-orange paints alternately to eight unmasked stripe areas. To discourage bleeding, run bristles flush against tape edge (illustration C). Remove tape while paint is still wet. Let dry 10 minutes, then apply additional coats free-hand as needed to fill gaps or eliminate streaking. Let dry at least 1 hour, but preferably overnight.

4. Mask and paint right diagonal stripes. Using triangle method from step 2, apply tape strips to container in right-fac-ing diagonal position, varying width of strips and spacing, to cre-ate eight new areas for stripes. Paint unmasked stripe areas as in step 3, alternating between green and fuchsia. Paint directly over previously painted stripes (illustration D). Remove tape and apply additional coats as in Step 3. Let dry at least 1 hour.

5. Paint stripe intersections. To create plaid effect, paint rec-tangular stripe intersections freehand using round brush; refer to sample plaid step-by-step (facing page). At each intersection, press wet brush in center of rectangle to shed excess paint, define cor-ners and edges using tip of brush, then fill in remainder of rectan-gle (illustration E). Let dry at least 1 hour, but preferably overnight.

6. Add finishing accents. Seal painted surface with shellac following manufacturer's instructions. Let dry 20 minutes.

Painting the Cachepot

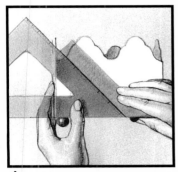

A. Press painter's tape against the cachepot, using a triangle as a guide.

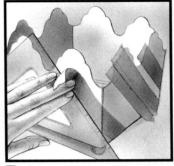

B. Vary the stripe widths and spacing as you continue the tape around the corners.

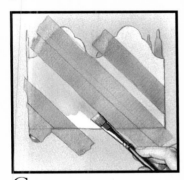

C. Paint the exposed areas between the strips of tape.

D. Repeat the previous steps to paint stripes in the opposite direction.

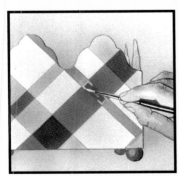

E. To create the plaid effect, paint each stripe intersection a contrasting color.

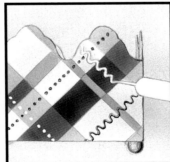

F. Use a paint syringe to apply small dots and very fine squiggly lines.

Transfer crimson, white, and periwinkle paint to individual paint syringes. Using syringes, paint the following: (1) a series of small white dots ¼in (6.4mm) in from left edge of three blue stripes, (2) a series of small crimson dots through center of three right-facing yellow stripes, (3) a squiggly crimson line through center of four right-facing yellow stripes, and (4) a squiggly white line through center of three left-facing yellow stripes (illustration F). Let painted dots and lines dry 20 minutes. Using round brush and working freehand, apply ⅛in (3.2mm) wide band of gold paint to lower edge and scalloped rim of container. Let dry 20 minutes. Apply tiny dots of pearlescent paint along lower edge and scalloped rim to camouflage irregularities. Turn container upside down and paint five gold stripes on each ball foot, then squeeze dots of periwinkle paint onto white areas in between. Let dry 1 hour. Seal container with two coats shellac.

Building the Plaid

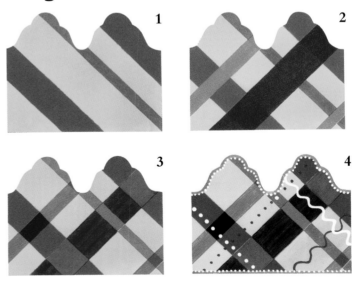

1. Create the left diagonal stripes using periwinkle and red-orange.

2. Then create the right diagonal stripes using green and fuchsia.

3. Paint the intersections of each stripe using the colors shown above.

4. To finish, add the dots and squiggly lines using a new set of colors.

lighting

Laminated Leaf Lampshade

This tasteful autumn leaf lampshade comes together beautifully and easily with only a few essential materials. When the lamp is lit, the laminated layers will unify into a soft, glowing pattern. To get started, you'll need to select a plain, paper-covered lampshade and an assortment of beautiful fall leaves or other foliage. To make the shade, glue the leaves onto the shade, then laminate them in place by gluing on a layer of translucent paper (e.g., Japanese mulberry paper). Finish the top and bottom edges of the lampshade with florist tape.

———

Red Velvet Candleshade

This elegant red velvet candleshade will dress up any dinner setting. At first glance, a candleshade might seem like a fire hazard. When using a candle follower (see diagram, page 41) and a straight (not tapered) candle, however, it's possible to safely display a shade on a lit candle. Making the shade involves four simple steps: Measuring your candle follower, drafting a template for the candleshade, covering the shade with velvet, and adding beads and a lining.

———

MATERIALS

- **Candle follower with harp**
- **12 x 12in (30.5 x 30.5cm) piece flocked red velvet**
- **12 x 12in (30.5 x 30.5cm) piece giftwrap paper**
- **Fifteen 10mm black glass beads**
- **Fifteen 2in (5cm) long pearl-head pins**
- **Lightweight bristol board**
- **Transparent stick-flat glue**

YOU'LL ALSO NEED:

compass; triangle; steel ruler; pencil; scissors; craft knife; self-healing cutting mat; newsprint; stiff brush (to apply glue); dressmaker's tape measure; 2 spring-clip clothespins; two ¾in (19.1mm) wide craft sticks; waxed paper; and heavy book.

Instructions
Making the Candleshade Arc

1. Draft basic candleshade arc. Measure harp height (a) and diameter (b) (see illustration A, at right). Following illustration B and working on bristol board, draft vertical line equal to harp height (a), then draft bisected perpendicular lines at each end, one equal to harp diameter (b) and one 6in (15.2cm) long, or what will be equal to diameter of lower shade (c). Draft two straight lines (d) through endpoints, extending them so they intersect at center point. Insert compass point at intersection and swing large and small arcs through endpoints. Multiply lower shade diameter (c) by 3.14 to determine lower shade circumference. Starting at outer edge, use tape measure to measure and mark this length around large arc (e). Draft straight line (f) connecting length mark to center point. Draft parallel line (g) ½in (12.7mm) away and connecting two arcs to indicate overlap.

2. Add guidelines for beads. Beginning at outer edge (d), measure and mark large arc in 1¼in (3.2cm) increments (illustration C). Align ruler on each mark and center point to draft fifteen 3in (7.6cm) long radial spokes.

3. Cut out arc template and lining. Lay bristol board on cutting mat. Cut out arc, using craft knife and steel ruler for straight edges and scissors for curved edges. Use arc as template to mark and cut lining from giftwrap, then set lining aside.
Note: Glue is applied in several of the following steps. To prevent glue from marring your project, place newsprint under your work and replace it with fresh sheets as the old ones become sticky. Use scrap bristol board to press and adhere the glued pieces.

4. Glue shade arc to velvet. Lay velvet right side down. Lay arc template marked side down on newsprint. Brush template with glue, going out beyond edges, then set arc glue side down on velvet and smooth. Trim excess velvet ½in (12.7mm) from edge all around, trim corners diagonally, and trim overlap edge even with arc straight edge (illustration D). Cut ¼in (6.4mm) slits ⅛in (3.2mm) apart on short curved edge, then cut notches ½in (12.7mm) apart along long curved edge. Brush glue onto each allowance, fold onto arc, and press (illustration E). Fold and glue down remaining straight edge allowance. Lay shade wrong side down on waxed paper, weight with heavy book, and let dry 1 hour.

Assembling the Shade

1. Shape and glue shade. Cut each of two craft sticks to equal shade height. Roll arc into shade shape so folded velvet edge overlaps trimmed edge by ½in (12.7mm), hold firmly, and test-fit on follower. Adjust width of overlap if needed, then using illustration F as a reference, sandwich overlapped section between splints and secure with clothespin at each end. Mark overlap edge on inside of shade. Undo clothespins, remove sticks, and let relax. Brush glue on overlap, reassemble, and reclip (illustration F). Let dry 2 hours.

2. Attach beaded trim. Insert pearl-head pin into black bead, then push pinpoint into shade rim even with radial line so shaft lodges within bristol board and black bead touches rim. Repeat to attach remaining beads evenly spaced all around (illustration G).

3. Glue in lining. Turn shade upside down. Test-roll lining and fit inside shade so straight edges align. Remove and trim curved edges, if necessary. With shade still upside down, brush glue inside top and bottom rims. Roll lining slightly tighter than necessary, insert it inside shade, then slowly unroll, pressing it against glue at each rim edge (illustration H). When you near starting point, brush glue on overlap and press down to adhere.

Making the Candleshade

A. Measure the candle follower's harp to determine the shade size.

B. To draft the basic shade arc, mark lines and arcs (a) through (g) on the bristol board.

C. Mark evenly spaced radial lines to indicate the bead placement.

D. Glue the shade arc to the velvet, trim the excess from the edges and corners, then clip and notch the allowances.

E. Glue the allowances to the shade arc so they lie flat.

F. Glue the shade seam and clip in place.

G. Attach the beads along the shade edge.

H. Position the lining inside the shade.

Fabric-Covered Lampshade

You've got a beautiful lamp, with a less-than-beautiful shade. Here's an easy way to incorporate the lamp into your decorating scheme: Cover the shade with fabric, perhaps to match a couch or a pillow. Start by cutting the existing shade off its wire rings, then use the cutoff shade as a template for creating a new shade from laminate paper. Attach your fabric to the laminate paper shade, which features a stiff paper backing for the shade on one side and peel-off adhesive on the reverse (no glue is necessary). To finish, trim the shade's edges with grosgrain ribbon, twisted cord, and fringe.

———

Seashell Candles

If you can boil water, you can make these beautiful seashell candles. All you need are large seashells, half a dozen old candle stubs, about 10in (25.4cm) of wire-core wick, an empty tin can, and a saucepan. Start by melting the candle stubs in a double boiler fashioned from the tin can and saucepan, then position a wick in each shell, and fill each shell with the melted wax. You can add scent to your candles using a few drops of scented oil, or color them using candle coloring. Arrange three or four of the seashell candles on a windowsill or use them as outdoor lighting on a porch or deck. For a quick and simple host or hostess gift, package a few candles together in a decorative box.

—

If you don't live near the beach, or the beach near you doesn't have any interesting seashells, try your local pet store, the bath department of a large department store, or a large craft store. Avoid shells with large holes or cracks; tiny openings, however, can be patched with white craft glue.

MATERIALS

- **Seashells, each 2–4in (5–1.20cm) across**
- **Candle stubs**
- **Flat wire-core wick, about 3in (7.6cm) per seashell**

YOU'LL ALSO NEED:

paring knife; cutting board; old saucepan; empty tin can to fit inside saucepan; needle-nose pliers; oven mitt and/or tongs; scissors; dishtowel; spoon; and newspaper or brown kraft paper.

OTHER ITEMS, IF NECESSARY:

white craft glue (for filling small holes or cracks in shells); scented oil (for scenting candles); and candle coloring (for tinting candles).

Instructions

1. Test shells for small holes. Fill each shell with water and watch for leaks. To plug small holes or cracks, dry shell with towel, then apply small amount of glue to hole or crack on outside of shell (see illustration A, facing page). Let glue dry completely per manufacturer's recommendations.

2. Melt wax for candles. Lay newspaper or kraft paper on kitchen counter convenient to stove, but not too close to burner. Set shells on work surface, making sure each is stable with cavity facing up. Bring 1in (2.5cm) water to boil in saucepan. Bend rim of tin can into V-shaped spout using pliers. Working on cutting board with paring knife, slice candle stubs into chunks no larger than ½in (12.7mm) across. Carefully place wax chunks in tin can. If tinting candles, add candle coloring to wax following manufacturer's instructions. Using tongs and/or oven mitt, lower can into boiling water (illustration B). Reduce heat to simmer until wax melts.

3. Add wicks to candles. Cut wick into 3in (7.6cm) sections. Spoon a few drops of hot liquid wax into shell basin (illustration C). Twist end of wick into circle and press into wax, adjusting wick so it stands upright (illustration D). Repeat to position wicks inside remaining shells.

4. Fill candles with wax. Using tongs and/or oven mitt, pour melted wax into each shell cavity (illustration E). To scent candle, add two or more drops scented oil to wax and mix before wax hardens. When candles are cool, trim excess wick within ½in (12.7mm) of wax surface (illustration F).

DESIGNER'S TIP

There are a variety of candlewicks on the market. For this project, we recommend flat wire-core wicks. Wire-core wick is made by braiding prepared cotton around a very thin wire core, which melts as the wick burns down. The main advantage to this type of wick is that the wire stiffens it, so it will stand by itself as you pour the wax around it. Wire-core wicks, like other types of wicks, come in three thicknesses. For candles this size, look for the W-1 thickness.

Making the Seashell Candles

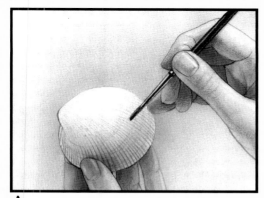

A. Seal small holes or cracks in the shell with white glue.

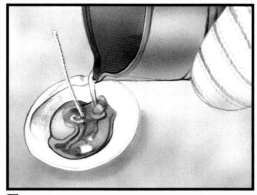

B. Place wax chunks in tin can, then simmer until fully melted.

C. Spoon a few drops of hot liquid wax into the shell basin.

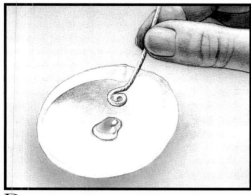

D. Curl one end of the wick and press it into the hot, soft wax.

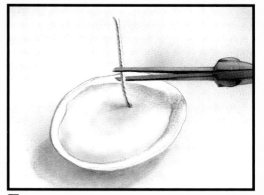

E. Once the wick is stable, fill the shell cavity with more wax.

F. Trim the wick when the wax is hard.

49

frames

Vintage Wallpaper Frame

It's no longer necessary to scour your local antique shop for a frame such as this one—now you can make your own for a fraction of the time and money. The distressed effect on this frame is created with two main materials: Crackle medium, which makes the frame's painted finish appear worn and chipped, and vintage wallpaper, which gives the piece its dated look. To create the antique finish, start by base-coating the frame with acrylic paint, then applying crackle medium and a second color of paint. The three layers will unite in a chipped, cracked effect. Next, cover the frame with wallpaper, then gently rip and scratch away small sections of the wallpaper to reveal the crackled paint underneath. Last, sand the edges and the frame's corners to smooth the transition between the paint and the paper, and to add to the worn look.

———

GUARANTEED 1197 RUN 3 NO 1950279

If you use a reproduction paper, look for one with a matte or low-sheen finish in order to make the frame look authentic. Vintage wallpapers have a very soft look, primarily a result of the color-screening process and the nonvinyl coating.

MATERIALS

- **Vintage wallpaper**
- **Flat, wide-border wooden frame**
- **2oz (59.2ml) acrylic paints (two colors; see steps 1 and 2)**
- **2oz (59.2ml) crackle medium**
- **2oz (59.2ml) matte acrylic sealer**
- **Wallpaper adhesive**

YOU'LL ALSO NEED:

hardwood seam roller or rolling pin; 150-grit sandpaper; two 1in (2.5cm) flat paintbrushes; craft knife; scissors; self-healing cutting mat; sponge; paper towels; and pencil.

DESIGNER'S TIP

Authentic vintage wallpaper can be expensive and hard to locate. For a less expensive alternative, consider ordering samples of reproduction vintage wallpaper through your local wallpaper store. Note: Some wallpaper dealers and manufacturers offer this option, and some don't. If you can find a dealer who does, however, it's a great source for this project and others requiring small amounts of wallpaper. Sample prices typically start at between $2 and $4.

Instructions

1. Paint basecoat color. For basecoat, choose accent color in wallpaper. Sand frame lightly. Remove dust with damp paper towel. Paint back, front, and inner and outer edges of frame. Let dry at least 1 hour, but preferably overnight. Clean brush in water.

2. Create crackle finish. Brush crackle medium onto face of frame and inner and outer edges. Let stand until surface turns tacky. Clean brush in water. For top coat, choose second accent color in wallpaper. Using dry brush, apply top coat paint over medium. Brush over each area only once, then let stand (see illustration A, facing page). Crackling action will begin immediately and intensify over next 20 to 30 minutes. Let dry at least 1 hour. Clean brush in water. When frame is dry, smooth surface by brushing on thin coat of sealer. Let dry overnight.

3. Glue wallpaper to frame. Gently sand face of frame, then wipe off dust with damp paper towel. On cutting mat, roll out wallpaper face up. Position frame on wallpaper, adjusting it to center patterns and stripes. Cut wallpaper approximately 1in (2.5cm) beyond frame edge (illustration B). If desired, lightly mark position of frame on paper for repositioning before adhesion. Remove frame and turn cut piece of wallpaper face down. Brush thin layer of wallpaper adhesive onto face of frame, then press frame in position face down onto back of wallpaper. Carefully turn frame over to make sure design is properly situated, reposition as necessary, then return face down. Wipe any oozing adhesive with paper towel. On cutting mat, run craft knife blade along inner and outer edges of frame to trim and remove excess paper (illustration C).

4. Create antique finish. Turn frame face up. Run roller or rolling pin along papered surface to press out air bubbles and ensure adhesion. Before adhesive dries completely, gently scratch or tear off small sections of wallpaper along inner and outer edges (illustration D). Wipe off lingering adhesive with damp sponge. Let dry overnight. Sand torn areas gently so they blend into painted surface. Sand frame corners and inner and outer edges to simulate wear.

Making the Wallpaper Frame

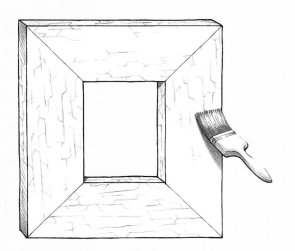

A. Paint the frame, using crackle medium between the coats for a weathered finish.

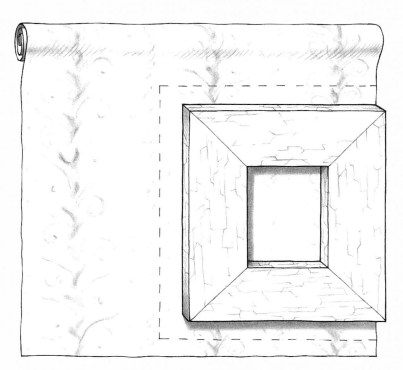

B. Cut a section of vintage wallpaper to fit the frame.

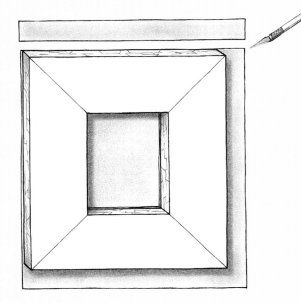

C. Glue the frame to the wallpaper, then trim away the excess.

D. Gently tear the wallpaper along the edges to expose the crackle finish.

Antique Brass Frames

These tarnished brass frames are not the antiques they appear to be. Replicating their oxidized and aged look, however, is a relatively quick process. Start by attaching stamped metal findings or corners to an ordinary brass frame, then imitate the effects of age with a bottled patinating formula. For best results with this project, shop for the findings first, then find a frame to match. Most findings measure between 1 and 1¾ in (2.5 to 4.4cm) wide, and look best on frames no larger than 5 x 7in (12.7 x 17.8cm).

———

A blue-green finish such as that shown on the frame at the far left is called verdigris. From the French word vert de Grece (green of Greece), it denotes the color of age. The mahogany tarnish on the other two frames mimics the look of antique brass.

MATERIALS

- **Brass frames, assorted shapes and sizes**
- **Brass findings, assorted shapes and sizes**
- **Patinating solution(s)**
- **Matte spray lacquer**
- **5-minute epoxy**

YOU'LL ALSO NEED:

protective eyewear; emery board; very fine (#0000) steel wool; paint stripper and/or acetone; toothpicks; disposable latex gloves; masking tape; dishwashing detergent; soft cloth; 1in (2.5cm) wide bristle paintbrush; paper towels; paper plates or index cards; and newspaper.

OTHER ITEMS, IF NECESSARY:

1in (2.5cm) disposable paintbrush, plastic food wrap, and old toothbrush (if using paint stripper); and cotton swabs or cotton balls (if using acetone).

Instructions
Preparing the Frames

Note: Always work in a well-ventilated area when using chemical solutions such as paint stripper, acetone, or patinating solution. Cover the workspace with newspaper and wear gloves and protective eyewear. Follow the manufacturer's instructions on all products.

1. Strip lacquer from frames. Remove backing, stand, and glass from frames and set aside. To remove lacquer from frames using paint stripper, apply stripper using disposable paintbrush. Wrap frame with plastic food wrap and set aside as indicated by manufacturer's instructions. Unwrap frame, then gently scrub softened lacquer from crevices using old toothbrush. To remove lacquer using acetone, dip cotton swab or cotton ball in acetone, then rub on frame surface. When lacquer is completely stripped, wash frame with dishwashing detergent and warm water, then dry with paper towels.

2. Affix findings to frame. Hold findings up to frames to determine positioning. To improve adhesion of findings, lightly abrade corresponding contact points on frames with tip of emery board. Mix epoxy on paper plate or index card following manufacturer's instructions. (Make about 1tsp [5ml] to start with, then make more as you run out.) Turn findings right side down. Use toothpick to fill in concave portion with epoxy, taking care not to let epoxy flow beyond edge of finding (see illustration A, facing page). Tape finding in place (illustration B) and

---

DESIGNER'S TIP

If the glass does not hold your photo snug in the frame, back the photo with several pieces of very thin cardboard.

Antiquing the Frame

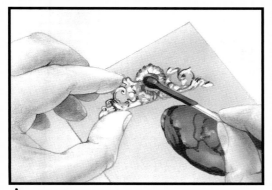

A. Fill in the concave area on the back of the finding with epoxy.

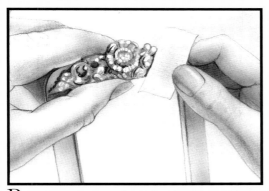

B. Press the finding in place, secure it with tape, and let it dry.

C. Apply the patinating solution to the frame using a clean bristle brush.

> ### DESIGNER'S TIPS
>
> You can use a variety of frame sizes and shapes for this project. Flat-faced frames work best because they provide a large flat area on which to glue the findings. You can use frames with curved faces if the points of contact form enough surface area to support the finding. Even poorly made frames with gaps at the corners can be used, as the findings will cover the gaps.
>
> Before applying the patinating solution, be sure to remove any lacquer on the frame with paint stripper or acetone. Even after this stripping process, however, some frames may still repel the patinating formula. In these cases, apply two coats of copper patinating solution, followed by an antiquing formula. You may have to experiment with your chosen frames, however, to get the desired results.

set aside to dry, frame face down, following epoxy manufacturer's instructions.

3. Antique frames. Remove tape from findings. Before proceeding, make sure findings are secure. Follow manufacturer's instructions to apply patinating solution(s) to frames using clean bristle paintbrush (illustration C). Complete patinating process, then let frames dry overnight. Use steel wool to highlight higher relief areas of findings. Use soft cloth to gently buff low areas of relief. For overall lighter finish, lightly buff entire frame with soft cloth.

4. Seal frames. Cover workspace with newspaper, then seal frames with coat of spray lacquer. Let dry completely following manufacturer's instructions. Restore glass, backing, and stand to frames.

Handmade Paper Frame

This elegant frame, assembled from handmade paper and chipboard, can be completed in an afternoon's time. The frame's flat, ample surface is ideal for displaying the most distinct characteristic of handmade paper: its rich, beautiful, and varied texture. To make the picture frame, you will need two to three sheets of 9 x 12in (22.9 x 30.5cm) light- to medium-weight handmade paper. Avoid extra thin or translucent papers, as the chipboard frame may shown through, or very thick sheets, which tend to break or crumble when folded.

—

Rose Petal Frame

This beautiful, delicate frame is decorated with dried rose petals. The roses are dried in silica gel crystals for several days, then attached to the frame using acrylic matte medium. Matte medium, a gummy, white liquid, softens the petals so they are more pliable and binds them permanently to the frame. The frame shown on facing page was decorated with petals from a solid-color rose, the peachy orange Sweetheart Porcelina. For a completely different look, the frame shown on page 68 was decorated with the petals of Sweetheart Minuette roses. To mimic the flower's natural growth pattern, the smallest petals are placed along the inner part of the frame, medium-sized petals in the middle, and large ones at the outer edge.

————

When you shop for a frame, look for one with a wide border to provide the most surface area to show off the petals. The frame we chose, measuring 6in (15.2cm) square with a 3in (7.6cm) square opening, required about 95 petals. Always dry more petals than you'll actually need because not all will be usable.

MATERIALS

- **6 x 6in (15.2 x 15.2cm) light-colored wooden picture frame with 3in (7.6cm) square opening**
- **1 dozen miniature roses**
- **8oz (236.8ml) acrylic matte medium**
- **3lbs (1.4kg) silica gel crystals**

YOU'LL ALSO NEED:

150-grit sandpaper; large, oblong container or airtight box with lid; soup spoon; slotted spoon or spatula; wire sieve or strainer; cookie sheet; round-edge burnisher or wooden dowel; 4in (10cm) wide acrylic brayer; brown kraft paper; blunt tweezers; soft, small round brush; paper plates; paper towels; waxed paper; goggles; particle mask; and disposable gloves.

OTHER ITEMS, IF NECESSARY:

electrician's tape (for sealing container).

Instructions

1. Dry petals in silica gel. For each rose, peel back sepals (green "prongs" at base of rose) and gently pull off petals one by one. Discard bruised or discolored petals. Set remaining petals aside. Put on goggles, mask, and gloves. Slowly pour thin, even layer of silica gel crystals into bottom of container or box. Lay petals in rows on crystals—close but not overlapping. Using soup spoon, sprinkle crystals over petals until all petals are completely covered. Place another layer of petals in box and sprinkle crystals to cover. Repeat until all petals are covered. Close container tightly; if lid does not form airtight seal, seal edge with tape. Let container rest undisturbed for 3 days.

2. Sort petals by size. On Day 3, open container and gently brush aside crystals so you can touch one petal with fingertip. If petal is still pliable, replace crystals on top and reseal container. Check again in same way on Day 4 and each succeeding day until petal is dry and stiff when touched. Put on goggles, mask, and gloves. Using slotted spoon or spatula, lift petals from crystals, transfer them to sieve or strainer, then gently shake to shed lingering crystals. Place preserved petals on cookie sheet. Sort through petals to select best-looking ones and arrange them by size in four groups: large, medium, small, and smallest.

3. Soften petals in matte medium. Cover work surface with kraft paper. Sand frame lightly to roughen surface for gluing. Pour 2–3in (5–7.6cm) wide puddle of matte medium onto

---

DESIGNER'S TIP

When selecting your roses, be sure to use only those roses with dry petals. If you apply silica gel to wet petals (such as those picked after a rainstorm or while the dew is still wet), the gel will stick to the petals, making removal more difficult. In addition, the desiccant will have to absorb so much extra moisture that its overall drying ability will be diminished.

paper plate. Select six to eight of the smallest petals and place them in medium. Use round brush to coat them lightly on both sides. Let petals sit 4–5 minutes or until soft and pliable. Check petals often, as oversoftening will make them difficult to handle. Continue softening petals in batches of six to eight as you need them for the following steps.

4. Position petals on sides of frame. Using tweezers, transfer softened petals to clean area of plate. Wipe off excess medium with brush. Pick up each petal individually with tweezers and position it with inner side of petal face up on frame. Start at inner corner and work your way around inner opening of frame, laying top one-third of petal on front inner edge and wrapping other two-thirds around to back of frame (see illustration A, below). Repeat to cover entire inner edge; as petals begin to dry, smooth them down with burnisher or dowel. Dab off excess medium with fingertip or paper towel. When edge is complete, lay waxed paper on glued frame and roll with brayer to eliminate air bubbles. Repeat process to affix smallest petals to outer edges of frame. Start at one corner, lay-

ing top one-quarter of each petal on front of frame, then wrapping petal around edge and onto back of frame (see illustration A). Burnish as before. Repeat to cover entire outer edge, then roll with brayer as before.

5. Cover front of frame. Soak large petals in medium as in step 3. Starting at any corner and working your way around frame, lay six or seven softened petals on frame side along outer edge of frame front using tweezers. Position petals so they are slightly touching each other and slightly overlapping the smallest petals already affixed (illustration B); burnish frame, then roll with brayer as above. Repeat process using medium-sized petals, positioning them to slightly overlap large petals (illustration B), then repeat using small petals, positioning them to overlap medium-sized petals and pressing excess onto edge of picture opening (illustration C).

6. Seal frame. When medium is fully dry (about 1 hour), place clean piece of waxed paper over frame front, weight with flat, heavy object, and let dry overnight. To seal petals completely, coat entire frame with light coat acrylic matte medium.

Attaching the Rose Petals

 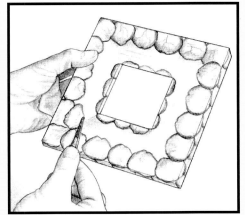 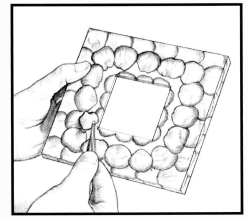

A. **Start by applying the very smallest of the rose petals to the frame's inner and outer edges.**

B. **Cover the outermost portion of the frame's front with the large petals, then fill in the second row with medium petals.**

C. **Fill in the innermost row with the small rose petals.**

furniture

Faux Marble Tabletop

Veined marble, characterized by distinct veins running over subtle color gradations, makes a beautiful faux finish for a tabletop. To create this effect, most professionals dip a goose feather in paint, then drag it across the table's surface, leaving veins of paint behind. The technique used to create this tabletop, however, is even simpler: Cover the tabletop with a coat of paint, followed by two different colors of glaze, then substitute your thumb for the goose feather. Wrap your thumb in cotton and drag it across the surface to remove "veins" of paint instead of adding them.

———

To achieve the most realistic marbled effect, select a smooth, grain-free surface for faux finishing, such as medium-density fiberboard (also known as MDF board), finer grades of plywood, or fiberboard. All of the above types of wood will need one or two coats of primer/sealer to prevent the wood from absorbing the basecoat.

MATERIALS

- **Medium-density fiberboard (or substitute)**
- **1qt (.95L) latex wood sealer**
- **1qt (.95L) semigloss black latex paint**
- **1qt (.95L) dark green latex paint**
- **1qt (.95L) teal green latex paint**
- **1qt (.95L) latex glaze**
- **Acrylic varnish**

YOU'LL ALSO NEED:

several lint-free cotton cloths about 16 x 16in (40.6 x 40.6cm) square; cheesecloth (machine-wash and dry before use); sandpaper grades 100 to 220; 400- and 600-grit wet-dry sandpaper; damp paper towels; foam brushes; plastic containers; old measuring cup or ladle; paint sticks; disposable gloves; tape measure; newspaper; and cotton cloth about 6 x 6in (15.2 x 15.2cm) square.

OTHER ITEMS, IF NECESSARY:

wood putty (to fill nicks in wood surface).

Instructions

Getting Started

1. Prepare and seal wood surface. If necessary, fill nicks with wood putty using finger. Let dry, then sand with 100-grit sandpaper and remove dust with damp paper towel. Repeat sanding and dust removal with increasingly finer grades of sandpaper to make wood as smooth as possible. Apply sealer with foam brush and let dry following manufacturer's recommendations. Sand lightly with 400-grit sandpaper, then remove dust with a damp paper towel. If wood still feels scratchy, apply second coat of sealer, let dry, and sand as above.

2. Apply basecoat and prepare glazes. Using foam brush, apply black paint basecoat following manufacturer's recommendations. Let dry thoroughly. When preparing paint-glaze mixtures, use separate container for each color. Allow 1 cup (.24L) glaze mixture for every 30 sq ft (2.79 sq m). Mix 3 parts glaze and 1 part dark green paint for dominant glaze, then repeat to mix 3 parts glaze and 1 part teal paint for secondary glaze.

Creating the Marbled Effect

Note: To allow glazes enough stay-wet time, work on no more than 9 sq ft (0.84 sq m) at a time. To prevent noticeable joins when glaze must be applied in sections, rub the wet glaze along the edges of each section until smooth and thin.

1. Apply glaze mixtures to wood. Put on disposable gloves. Using crumpled 16in (40.6cm) square of cotton cloth, apply glaze mixtures across wood in downward diagonal drift; apply dominant color to about 70 percent of surface and secondary color to about 30 percent of surface (see illustration A, facing page). Vary touch so glaze is thick in some areas and thin in others (illustration A, dotted and solid lines) with a hint of basecoat showing through. To tone down and blend glaze colors, press cheesecloth against wet surface.

2. Make first vein. Wrap 6in (15.2cm) square of cotton cloth around thumb, holding excess bulk in palm. Starting at far edge, put thumb into wet glaze and pull it diagonally across surface, passing through thinly glazed areas, to remove some glaze. To avoid making vein too straight, jiggle hand every few inches to create craggy shift in line, then continue along same diagonal path (illustration B). To vary vein thickness, use pad of thumb to remove wider band of glaze and side of thumb to remove thinner band of glaze. As glaze collects on thumb, periodically wipe excess on newspaper.

3. Make additional veins. Start 4–5in (10.2–12.7cm) from first vein in another thinly glazed spot. Draw this second vein diagonally in same manner as first, angling it so it intersects first vein. Draw second vein along first vein for 1–2in (2.5–5.1cm), then break off from first vein and continue on in original second vein direction (illustration C). For realistic look, add two or three additional veins in lightly glazed areas; make between four and six veins total. If glaze becomes too tacky to work, dampen thumb cloth with water. To make some veins appear deep and recessed, dab veins with cheesecloth.

4. Let glazed surface dry at least 4 hours, but preferably overnight. Using foam brush to prevent bubbles, apply acrylic varnish to entire surface. Let dry 1 hour or as manufac-turer recommends. When dry, sand lightly with 600-grit sandpaper and remove dust with damp paper towel. For strong, durable finish, apply total of four to five coats of varnish, sanding lightly with 600-grit sandpaper and removing dust between coats.

Color Variation

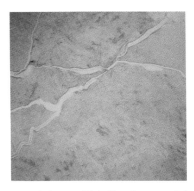 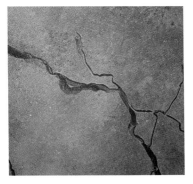

For a lighter marbled effect, shown top left, substitute a cream-colored basecoat, followed by a dominant glaze of peach paint and a secondary glaze of gray paint. The finish shown on the right was created with a dark palette: Start with a black basecoat, followed by glazes mixed from dark green (dominant) and teal (secondary) paints.

Creating the Marbled Effect

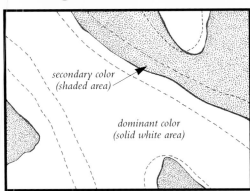

A. Apply the two glazes in a downward diagonal drift. Within the glazed area, include thick (solid lines) and thin (dotted lines) areas.

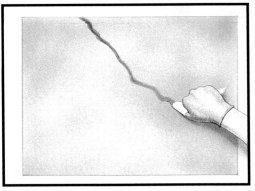

B. To make the first vein, pull on a glove, wrap your thumb with cotton cloth and drag it across the glazed surface.

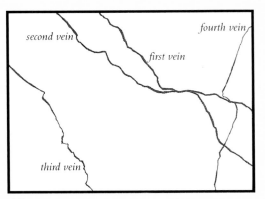

C. For a realistic look, make two veins intersect and travel together for 1–2in (2.5–5.1cm) before breaking them off.

Farmhouse Table

Say "rustic country faux finish," and most people think of chipped and peeling paint. This table, however, features a softer patina. By using layers of varnish, paint, and glaze, and gentle sanding in between, you can create the look of a 1930s farmhouse table that has aged slowly and gracefully. The colors you select should be fresh and lively, but not too sharp. For a kitchen table such as this, try to echo the colors of the appliances and furnishings of that time; a sample palette includes pea green, bluish green, and ivory. The use of these colors, combined with the aging effect, makes the table appear as though, given a good scrubbing, it would look fresh and new.

——

For this faux finish, we recommend water-based paints and varnish because they dry quickly. In addition, remove the legs from the table before finishing them to provide easier access.

MATERIALS

- Unfinished wooden table
- 1qt (.95L) latex primer
- 1qt (.95L) ivory matte latex paint
- 1qt (.95L) yellow-green matte latex paint
- 1qt (.95L) blue-green matte latex paint
- 1qt (.95L) latex satin varnish
- ½ cup (118ml) latex glaze
- ½ cup (118ml) brown matte latex paint

YOU'LL ALSO NEED:

120- and 180-grit sandpaper; drop cloth; cotton cloths; 1in (2.5cm) and 2in (5.1cm) natural bristle paintbrushes; paint sticks; 1pt (.47L) plastic container; paper towels; spray mister; 2in (5.1cm) wide painter's tape; craft knife; measuring cup; and steel ruler.

Instructions

1. Sand and prime table. Protect work area with drop cloth. Sand table lightly with 120-grit sandpaper, following wood grain. Remove dust with lightly misted paper towel. Brush on primer, then let dry 1 hour, or follow manufacturer's recommendations.

2. Apply "sloppy" varnish coat. To simulate years of paint buildup, brush varnish onto table in sloppy, uneven coat that is thick in some areas and thin in others. Do not remove rings, sags, or bubbles. Before varnish dries, apply second coat in same "sloppy" fashion over approximately 40 percent of table. Let dry at least 1 hour longer than manufacturer recommends, but preferably overnight.

3. Paint ivory and green layers. Brush even coat of ivory paint over entire table. Let dry 1 hour longer than manufacturer recommends. Using 180-grit sandpaper, sand back ivory paint in raised areas to partially expose varnish layer underneath, then remove dust. Using cotton cloth, rub yellow-green paint into wood along grain and let dry 1–2 hours. Sand back portions of yellow-green layer to suggest layer of paint that has worn off over time (see illustration A, facing page).

4. Paint ivory border striping. Press painter's tape around

DESIGNER'S TIP

When choosing a furniture style of the 1930s, keep in mind that it falls between the highly decorative trend of the early part of the century and the sleek, modern furniture styles of the late forties and fifties. The lines of the table should be fairly straightforward, with minimal shaping in the legs.

perimeter of tabletop, even with edge, to form large rectangle. To create border stripe, press down additional tape parallel to first tape, allowing ¼ in (6.4mm) space between them. Run craft knife against ruler to trim excess tape at corners. Using cloth, rub ivory paint in ¼ in (6.4mm) space between tape strips. Rub ivory paint into outermost edge of tabletop and one or two turnings on each leg.

5. Paint green interior. Using damp, crumpled cotton cloth, randomly dab blue-green paint onto table area bordered by inner tape. To create texture, allow the pattern created by the crumpled cotton cloth to show (illustration B). Remove tape and let dry 2 hours.

6. Apply "dirty" aging glaze. Mix ½ cup (118ml) glaze and ½ cup (118ml) brown paint together in pint container. Dip lightly misted cotton cloth into mixture, then rub glaze onto all surfaces for an overall "dirty" patina (illustration C). Let dry 2

hours. Sand lightly and unevenly with 180-grit sandpaper, following wood grain, then remove dust as before. Finish with two light, even coats of varnish, letting dry 1 hour between coats. Let dry overnight.

DESIGNER'S TIP

The paint colors used in this project can be easily changed to give the table a particular look. A Shaker palette, for instance, might use terracotta paint layered on top of gray paint, cream on pale blue, or pale blue on terracotta. A Scandinavian palette would use blue-gray on ivy green, green on stone, gray on pale blue, or coral on umber.

Color Development

A. Apply ivory basecoat to table. Rub in yellow-green paint, then sand to expose the layer underneath.

B. Stencil an ivory border stripe and add blue-green accents.

C. To create a "dirty" patina, rub a brown glaze mixture over all the surfaces.

English Manor Ottoman

This ottoman, designed for the beginning furniture maker, can be assembled using five basic tools: a drill, a saw, a staple gun, a hammer, and scissors. The ottoman is constructed from two primary components: a seat and legs. The seat consists of a plywood rectangle reinforced on the underside with pine boards. The top of the seat is upholstered with a plump layer of foam, followed by the decorative fabric of your choice. The legs are actually curtain rod finials that are attached to the seat with hanger bolts, rather than wood screws, to give them more stability. The complicated joinery, webbing, and tied springs used for traditional upholstery have been replaced with an assembly of ready-cut wood parts and high-density foam.

—

Country Stripe Cupboard

This festive striped cupboard makes a beautiful holiday shelf for special ornaments or Christmas decorations. You can start with an unfinished cupboard and paint two sets of contrasting stripes, or select a finished piece, like the distressed green cupboard shown at right, and add just one set of stripes. To give the cupboard a special finishing touch, add very thin gold stripes using a gold marker. The finished cupboard is neat but not fussy, with a festive folk art charm.

———

C. Paint the areas between the tape strips.

D. Peel up all the remaining pieces of tape to reveal the striped design.

87

Instructions

decorative items

Classic Carriage Clock

The design of this carriage clock pays homage to its early 1900s inspiration, then adds a modern twist. The clock case, made from a hinged basswood box, features a classic clock face accented with Roman numerals, and brass hardware. To update the design, the clock body is covered with faux shagreen, or shark-skin, paper. This choice is in keeping with the clock's 1920s look: During the early 1900s, genuine shagreen was dyed in many colors and veneered onto small items such as matchboxes and desk sets. The finished clock is sleek and clean, suitable for a wide range of decorating styles.

———

For variation on this design, substitute red faux crocodile paper.

MATERIALS

- 26 x 40in (66 x 101.6cm) green faux shagreen paper
- 3 x 5 x 6½in (7.6 x 12.7 x 16.5cm) basswood box
- 2⅞in (7.3cm) Roman clock face and works
- 1.5-volt battery
- Brass bail pull handle
- 4 brass feet
- Small brass latch
- Ivory spray paint
- Cyanoacrylic glue

YOU'LL ALSO NEED:

drill and bits; coping saw; 180-grit sandpaper; 400-grit wet-dry sandpaper; sanding block; scrap wood blocks; steel ruler; craft knife with new blade; self-healing gridded cutting mat; scissors; 3/4in (19.1mm) stencil brush; newsprint; pencil; compass; tape; paper towels; spray mister; full laundry detergent bottle; thick rubber band; table knife; hammer; nails; and screwdriver.

Instructions

Marking and Cutting the Box

1. Mark hardware positions on box. For clock face, lay box lid side down with hinges at right. Draft very light pencil line 2⅝in (6.7cm) from top edge, mark midpoint, then set compass point at midpoint and scribe 2¼in (5.7cm) diameter circle or to match radius at back of clock face (see illustration A, facing page). For bail pull, stand box on end with circle near top. Lightly draft centered perpendicular lines across both halves of box top surface, dividing box top into quarters. Position bail pull on longer line (on the portion of the box that will contain the clock face) and mark position with two dots (illustration A). For feet, turn box over so opposite end faces up. Mark line ½in (12.7mm) in from each edge at corners.

2. Drill holes at markings. To prevent wood from splitting, open box and support drilling area from behind with blocks of scrap wood. For circle, drill ½in (12.7mm) diameter starter hole at center using either bit, then use coping saw to cut along marked line. Drill bail pull holes with ⅛in (3.2mm) bit and feet holes with 3⁄32in (2.4mm), or appropriate size, bit.

Painting the Box

1. Prepare surface for painting. Using 180-grit sandpaper on sanding block, lightly sand all surfaces of box with grain, taking care not to round corners. Remove dust with damp paper towel.

2. Spray-paint box ivory. Follow spray paint manufacturer's recommendations to set up painting area. Place opened box on laundry detergent bottle. Spray two to three coats ivory paint across entire outside surface and inside rims; allow 5 to 10 minutes drying time between coats. Let dry overnight. Sand lightly with 400-grit wet-dry sandpaper on sanding block. Apply two final coats of spray paint, concentrating on edges for smooth, even finish. Let dry overnight.

Papering and Finishing the Box

1. Cut shagreen panels. Using ruler, craft knife with new blade, and cutting mat, cut 6 x 40in (15.2 x 101.6cm) strip of shagreen, then make perpendicular cuts (at precise right angles) to yield five 6 x 8in (15.2 x 20.3cm) panels. In steps that follow, position each panel so right-angle cut fits into box corner.

2. Glue and trim back panel. Lay one shagreen panel face down on newsprint. Using stencil brush, apply glue in circular motion across back of panel and out beyond edges. Lay box so clock face opening faces down. Set shagreen panel, glue side down, onto surface and ease into position until right-angle cut is 1/16in (1.6mm) from box edges, revealing thin white band along two edges (illustration B). Press shagreen panel into position and smooth with palm. Trim opposite corner diagonally with scissors to expose sliver of white box corner beneath (illustration B). Lay steel ruler on box, aligning it 1/16in (1.6mm) in from exposed corners at each end, and trim off excess side panel with craft knife. Repeat to trim bottom edge. Wipe glue from surface and edges with damp paper towel.

3. Glue and trim top panels. Open box and stand upright.

DESIGNER'S TIP

Wondering why you need to paint the entire box, when only a thin pinstripe edge is visible on the finished project? The spray-paint coating protects the wood and forms a smooth surface onto which the paper can be evenly glued.

Marking the Box

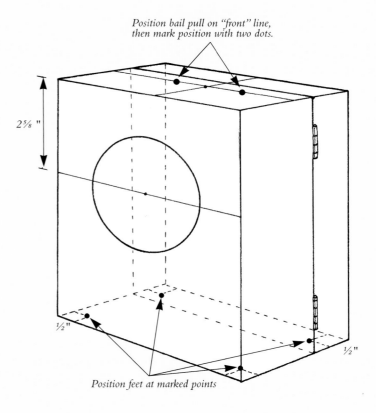

Position bail pull on "front" line, then mark position with two dots.

2⅝"

½"

½"

Position feet at marked points

A. Mark, drill and saw openings in a basswood box to accommodate the clock face and accompanying hardware.

Cut one panel in half lengthwise, then glue one piece to bail pull section, exposing thin white band around three edges as in Step 2 (illustrations C and D). Carefully poke nail tip through predrilled holes for bail pull. Turn box right side up. Crease flap against inside rim, close box against flap, and secure with rubber band (illustration D). Trim panel side edges as in Step 2 to expose 1/16 in (1.6mm) white trim. Open box, clip flap corners diagonally with scissors as shown in illustration E, then glue flap onto rim and inside box. Repeat process to trim and glue second piece of shagreen to remaining box top area.

4. Glue and trim unhinged side panels. Stand box hinged side down. Cut one panel in half lengthwise. Trim and glue pieces to unhinged side of box, as for top panels in Step 3.

5. Glue and trim hinged side panels. Stand box hinged side up. Cut one panel in half lengthwise and glue one piece in position as in Step 2. Trim excess 1/2 in (12.7mm) beyond box spine with scissors. To make cutouts around hinges, clip into flap until you reach hinge ends (a total of four clips), then run craft knife along hinge barrel to connect clips. Remove cutouts, press panel flat against box, and trim remaining panel edge (illustration F). Open box, clip flap corners, slip exposed flaps to inside, and glue to box rim and interior as in Step 3. Trim and glue other piece to remaining area in same way (illustration G).

6. Glue and trim front panel. Glue and trim front panel as for back panel, Step 2. Open box, lay it face down on mat, and use craft knife to cut panel to within 1/4 in (6.4mm) of circumference of circle cutout. Notch this allowance every 1/4 in (6.4mm) all around, then press tabs onto cutout rim. Apply additional glue to flaps if necessary. Let dry 3 hours.

7. Attach latch, feet, and bail pull. Hold box closed with rubber band, and stand so painted surface (bottom of clock) faces up. Position closed latch on box so it straddles seam, and tape down. Tap in nails (provided by manufacturer) to secure, then remove tape. Screw in feet at predrilled holes. Turn clock right side up and attach bail pull using nuts provided. Metal rods should extend down into box. To install clock face, insert battery behind clock face and push clock face into circle cutout (illustration H).

Assembling the Clock

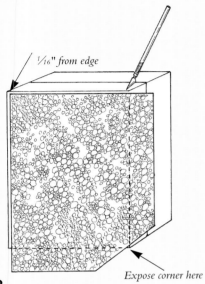

¹⁄₁₆" from edge

Expose corner here

B. **Glue a shagreen panel to the box back, leaving a thin white band exposed along two edges.**

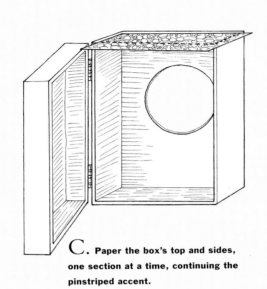

C. **Paper the box's top and sides, one section at a time, continuing the pinstriped accent.**

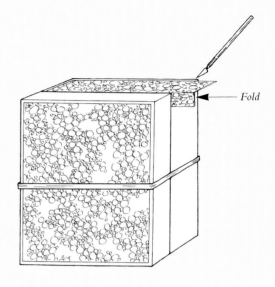

Fold

D. **Fold the excess paper to the inside, hold the box closed with a rubber band, and trim the side edge.**

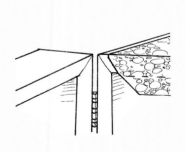

E. **On the inside of the box, trim the flaps diagonally, then glue them to the box rim.**

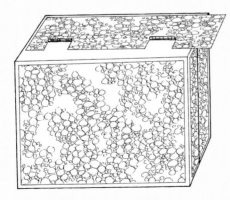

F. **Cut openings in the flap to fit one panel snugly around the hinges.**

G. **Glue the flap sections that remain to the inside rim, bypassing the hinges.**

Foot

H. **Cut an opening in the front panel's paper, then attach the hardware and insert the clock face.**

95

Home Sweet Home Sign

Although this sign looks as though it came right out of an 19th-century farm-house, it was created using modern materials and techniques. The project is made in two general stages: constructing the sign first, and then adding the antique finish. The sign is made from a plain pine plank and the raised letters are actually self-adhesive wooden letters. To define the edges of the sign and make a frame for the letters, we used molding around the sign's edges. Creating the aged finish involves three different steps: painting and crackling the undercoats, gilding and aging the letters, and applying a final wash of diluted ivory-colored paint.

———

The directions provided with this project could be used to make a small door sign for a child's room or a "Welcome to Our Home" sign.

MATERIALS

- 1½in (3.8cm) self-adhesive wooden letters, 1 package each (each package contains two letters) H, O, M, S, W, T and 2 packages E
- 1 package self-adhesive small wooden hearts
- Clear pine board measuring 24 x ¾ x 9½in (61 x 1.9 x 24.1cm)
- 6ft (1.8m) ⅜ x ¼in (9.5 x 6.4mm) beaded glass molding
- ½in (12.7mm) brads
- Acrylic paint, 2oz (59.2ml) each in the following colors: gloss enamel black, twill, ivory white, parchment, and rust
- 2oz (59.2ml) antique gold acrylic paint
- 2oz (59.2ml) crackle medium
- Matte acrylic sealer spray
- Wood glue

YOU'LL ALSO NEED:

pattern for sign arc (see page 121); access to photocopier with enlarger; transfer paper (do not use carbon paper); pencil; grid ruler; miter box; backsaw with closely spaced teeth; 180-grit sandpaper; sanding block; tack hammer; 5 paintbrushes in the following sizes: #3 round, ¼in (6mm) flat, ½in (12.7mm) flat, and 1in (2.5cm) flat, small round brush or cotton swab; paper towels; spray mister; small cup; and cellulose sponge.

Instructions

Constructing the Sign

1. Join molding strips to board. Lightly sand surface and edges of board, removing dust with damp paper towel. Lay board flat. Using grid ruler and pencil, draft line ⅛in (3.2mm) in from each edge to make rectangle. From molding, cut two 23¾in (60.3cm) strips and two 9¼in (23.5cm) strips, mitering ends 45° picture frame-style. Test-fit strips along guidelines allowing ⅛in (3.2mm) rim all around. Start three brads partway, and at an angle, into each shorter strip and five brads into each longer strip. Apply glue to board along line, then on each strip bottom. Reposition strips on board and tap down brads flush with molding surface (see illustration A, facing page).

2. Affix letters and heart to board. Photocopy arc pattern shown on page 121. Center pattern on board and slip transfer paper under. Lightly trace center line, arc guideline, and heart outline (do not trace letters). Remove pattern. Referring to pattern and starting at center of board, arrange letters on guideline in each direction to spell HOME SWEET HOME (illustration B). Starting at center, peel off backing and press each letter into position. Work carefully because letters cannot be repositioned once they are adhered. Adhere heart within outline. Sand lightly to remove any visible tracing lines.

Painting the Sign

1. Paint basecoats. Using 1in (2.5cm) flat brush for large areas and ½in (12.7mm) brush around letters, apply ivory white paint to entire board, including edges. Let dry 1 hour. Brush twill paint onto open areas of sign in smudgy, irregular patches (illustration C). Let dry at least 1 hour, but preferably overnight. Clean brushes using soap and water.

2. Paint crackle finish. Using ½in (12.7mm) flat brush, apply crackle medium randomly over open areas of sign, includ-

Making the Sign

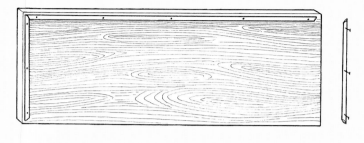

A. To construct the sign, miter-cut strips of molding and fasten them to the edges of the pine plank with glue and brads.

B. Arrange the self-stick wooden letters on the curved guideline, working from the center outward.

C. Paint the entire surface, then add random splotches of a second color.

D. Use crackle medium and another paint layer to antique the surface.

ing between words. Vary application so some areas receive thicker coat than others. Let dry to touch, 10–15 minutes. Using 1in (2.5cm) flat brush for large areas and ½in (12.7mm) brush around letters, apply parchment paint to entire surface, brushing with wood grain. Set aside board; do not attempt touch-ups. Areas coated with crackle medium will begin crackling right away and be completed in about 20 minutes (illustration D). Let dry overnight. Clean brushes using soap and water.

3. Paint and gild letters and molding. Using ¼in (6.4mm) flat brush, paint surface of letters with two coats black and surface of heart with two coats rust. Using round brush, paint molding black. Let dry 20 minutes. Using ¼in (6.4mm) flat brush and working one word at a time, apply thin layer of crackle medium to letters. When medium is dry to touch, 10 minutes or less, brush on gold paint. As soon as gold surface begins to crackle, dab with moistened paper towel to lift and remove gold flecks. Apply crackle medium, then gold paint, to beaded section of molding in same way. Rub towel along length of strips to break up gold into streaks. Finally, use round brush to paint ⅛in (3.2mm) gold border around edge of heart. Let dry at least 1 hour, but preferably overnight. Clean brushes using soap and water.

4. Apply ivory wash. Following manufacturer's recommendations, spray sign with two coats acrylic sealer. Let dry 3 hours, but preferably overnight. To make wash, dilute 1tbsp (14.8ml) ivory white paint with one or two drops water. Using round brush, work wash into crevices and up sides of letters. Blot up excess with damp paper towel and/or damp sponge. Brush wash onto molding, then sponge off beaded portion. Finally, use 1in (2.5cm) flat brush to apply wash to remaining flat areas. Blot with paper towel. Let dry 1 hour. Clean brushes using soap and water.

Faux Limoges Hinged Boxes

Purchased in a gift shop or by catalog, an authentic porcelain Limoges box might cost upwards of $100. You can create your own faux-limoge reproductions using heat-set resin clay and china paints, however, for about one-tenth the cost. Though the pear, lime, and peach designs shown here could never pass for real Limoges, their lifelike coloring, hinged cavities, and wire-trimmed edges create an easy make-at-home reproduction.

———

You can use the directions provided here to make a variety of other fruit, such as oranges, plums, lemons, melons, or apples.

MATERIALS

- **Heat-set modeling clay (about 2oz [56.8g] per fruit)**
- **1oz (29.6ml) nonfiring acrylic stains in the following colors:**
  Lime: green olive, medium green, and cinnamon
  Peach: French vanilla, pumpkin, boysenberry, and cinnamon
  Pear: yellow haze, camel, and cocoa brown
- **Modeling clay glossy glaze**
- **½ x ½in (12.7 x 12.7mm) brass hinge(s)**
- **Narrow flat brass wire or metallic cord (about 12in [30.5cm] per fruit)**
- **Granulated sugar**
- **Cyanoacrylic glue**

YOU'LL ALSO NEED:

1¼in (3.2cm) diameter wooden balls (one per fruit); cookie sheet; clay sculpting tools; needle-nose pliers; wire cutters; metal nail file; 400-grit wet-dry emery paper; craft knife; nylon round, stippling, and fine-tipped paintbrushes; old toothbrush; plastic palette; paper towels; cellulose sponge; dinner plate; dark-colored polyester thread; and laundry detergent bottle.

OTHER ITEMS, IF NECESSARY:

broomstick (to preshape brass wire).

Instructions

1. Make basic clay ball. Knead 2oz (56.8g) clay until soft. Roll clay into 1½in (3.8cm) diameter ball, then press thumb into ball to form bowl. Insert wooden ball into bowl and manipulate clay until ball is completely covered with clay (see illustration A, facing page).

2. Form fruit. Model each fruit individually as directed below, then proceed immediately to Steps 3 and 4 while clay is still soft. Bake all fruits together (Step 5).

Lime: Pinch opposite ends of ball (illustration B) to make two points, then press points against palm to dull and swell tips (illustration C). Carefully press lime against plate at 45° angle to flatten one side for base. Use fingers to press ⅛in (3.2mm) thick layer of granulated sugar into surface to create dimpled texture.

Peach: Pinch bottom of ball, then press in on opposite end to form dimple (illustration D). Smooth dimple so rim curves gently into sides of fruit and sharpen point so overall fruit resembles a peach (illustration E). Using flat-edged sculpting tool, imprint arching crease from top dimple down side of fruit, ending in whorling dent at bottom tip. To accentuate crease, press in along one side so edge swells out, then smooth ridges to round out swells (illustration F). Roll small bit of clay to resemble rice grain and press into dimple for stem.

Pear: Knead and roll ½in (12.7mm) diameter ball of clay until very soft, then press onto basic clay ball (illustration G, page 105). Smooth where the two balls join, then tilt appendage slightly to one side to form pear shape (illustration H). Taper bottom half of pear, then press thumb into larger end of pear to create dimple about ½in (12.7mm) wide by ⅛in (3.2mm) deep. Press dimpled end onto plate to flatten base so pear stands upright. Use round-pointed sculpting tool to make small dimple in top of pear. Roll

Forming the Lime, Peach, and Pear

Basic Ball

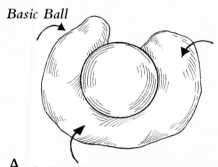

A. To shape the box cavity, roll a ball of clay, then embed a wooden ball within it.

Lime

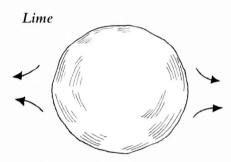

B. To form the lime, pinch and draw out the opposite ends of the basic ball.

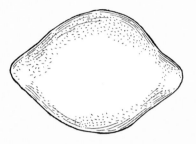

C. Press down on the pointed ends to dull and round the tips.

Peach

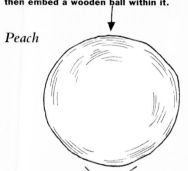

D. Pinch and draw out the bottom of the ball and press it in at the top to form a dimple.

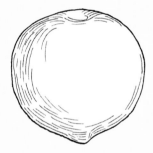

E. Smooth the top dimple and sharpen the pointed tip.

F. Use a clay sculpting tool to add a gently curving ridge, then add a clay stem.

Pear

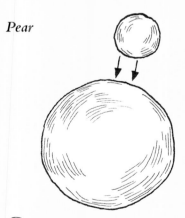

G. Press a small clay ball onto the basic ball.

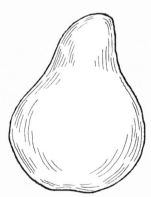

H. Smooth the join, then shape and taper the added section.

I. Taper the base, press a dimple at the pear's bottom, and add a stem at the top.

small bit of clay to resemble rice grain and set into dimple for stem (illustration I).

3. Slice fruits with thread. Wrap length of polyester thread around waist of each fruit one and one-half times, then pull thread ends gently in opposite directions, cinching through clay until you reach wood core (illustration J). To remove thread, release one end and pull other end through slowly until it comes out clean.

4. Embed hinge in fruit. Using thumbnail, mark hinge position at back of fruit along sliced line. Carefully lift up top hemisphere of fruit, leaving wooden ball lodged in bottom half of fruit. Open hinge 60° and push lower half of hinge into bottom

---

DESIGNER'S TIP

Each of the faux Limoges fruits has a different color story. The key to creating a realistic effect is to layer the colors of paint, applying them with different textural methods. These include sponging and ragging, which leaves mottled patterns, and stippling, which leaves tiny flecks, such as the spots on a pear.

---

hemisphere of fruit at 30° angle until hinge spine lodges against rim of fruit. Push top hemisphere onto other half of hinge, then lower top hemisphere of fruit back onto ball (illustration K). Smooth clay around hinge flanges using fingers.

5. Bake fruit in oven. Preheat oven to 275°F (140°C), Place fruit on cookie sheet, set in oven, and bake 30–45 minutes. Remove from oven. Let cool 20–30 minutes, or until moderately warm. Gently separate two halves of fruit, slicing through stuck areas with craft knife. Remove ball. Take care not to twist or distort the fruit. Check hinge operation and file clay that prevents easy movement. When completely cool, sand or file off fingerprints and blemishes. If hinge is loose, inject cyanoacrylic glue into join from inside box. Let dry following manufacturer's directions.

6. Paint individual fruits. Using paintbrushes, apply stains/china paints to fruit surface, then sponge off or manipulate colors as directed below. Prop each fruit open on laundry detergent bottle for initial coats but close fruit for final sponging or stippling across crack. Mix colors in plastic palette. To create loose stippled effect, moisten stippling brush with paint, dab excess on paper towel until bristles are almost dry, then tamp on fruit surface. For coarse stippling, load stippling brush or toothbrush (for more extreme effect) with paint, then draw fingertip across bristles to spatter paint onto fruit. When done, let paint dry at least 30 minutes.

Lime: Using round brush, paint entire surface and inside rims with medium green, then blot with damp sponge to lighten texture. Apply loose stipple with green olive paint, then blot lightly. Using fine-tipped brush, mix 1 drop each green olive and cinnamon, then paint five-pointed star at top for stem nub.

Peach: Using round brush, paint entire surface and inside rims with French vanilla. To suggest sun ripening, apply pumpkin in coarse stipple over fruit surface using stippling brush, then use damp sponge to blot up pumpkin and expose French vanilla on "shade" side of fruit. Mix 1 drop each boysenberry and cinnamon and brush over "sun-exposed" side. Smooth and blend edges with damp sponge, then streak off color by running dry crumpled paper towel across wet surface. Repeat to intensify blush. Paint stem using cinnamon.

Pear: Using round brush, paint entire surface and inside rims with yellow haze, then blot with damp sponge for soft mottling. To suggest sun ripening, brush camel on one side of fruit, from bottom to crown. Feather edges with dry brush, then dab with dry crumpled paper towel to soften and blend color. Apply coarse stippling using stippling brush or toothbrush and cocoa brown as desired. While paint is still wet, press damp sponge onto surface to soften stipples. Using fine-tipped brush and cocoa brown, paint stem and five-pointed star at base.

7. Apply glaze. Prop fruit open on detergent bottle. Using round brush, apply two thin coats glaze to outer surface, working each half separately. Let dry 20 minutes between coats.

8. Apply rims. If using wire, preshape it by winding it tightly around broomstick, then let it spring open. For each fruit, cut two wire or cord lengths to fit around each rim, beginning and ending at hinge. Bend wire gently by hand to fit curves of each fruit's two rims, taking care not to chip clay surface. Use needle-nose pliers to crease peach rim to match crease in fruit. Following manufacturer's recommendations, affix wire or cord to rim using cyanoacrylic glue. Let dry following manufacturer's recommendations.

Adding the Hinge

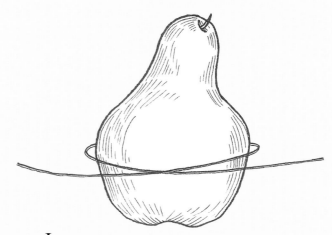

J. Slice the molded fruit in two using a length of thread.

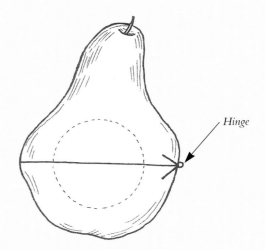

Hinge

K. Embed the hinge into the two halves at an angle for a firm join.

105

Frosted Perfume Bottles

This project uses what some people call the Cinderella principle: start with an ordinary glass flask, then use everyday craft materials to turn it into a beautiful, decorative perfume bottle. To achieve this transformation, you'll need etching cream for creating the frosted effects, aluminum leafing for a rich, metallic finish, and glass cabochons (flatsided, faceted beads) for several drops of jewellike color.

—

The ideal bottles for this project should be made of clear glass and have little to no surface decoration. Bottles with heavy casting seams (usually visible at the sides), should not be leafed, as the metallic foil will only emphasize those areas. Such bottles can be frosted, however.

MATERIALS

Cylinder Bottle
- Small bottle with glass stopper
- 1 sheet aluminum leaf
- Gold glass paint
- 2 oz (59.2ml) bottle etching cream
- 2 oz (59.2ml) bottle japan size
- 4 oz (118.4ml) bottle clear glaze

Ovoid Bottle
- Ovoid bottle with glass stopper
- 7 to 10 5mm round cabochons
- 1 sheet composition gold leaf
- Gold glass paint
- 2 oz (59.2ml) bottle etching cream
- 2 oz (59.2ml) bottle japan size
- 4 oz (118.4ml) bottle clear glaze
- Fabric glue

YOU'LL ALSO NEED:

¼in (6.4mm)-, ½in (1.3cm)-, and 1in (2.5cm)-wide masking tape; ⁵⁄₁₆in (7.9mm)-diameter self-stick circles; #4 round sabeline brush; ¾in (1.9cm)-wide foam brush; butter knife; cotton swab; rubber gloves; safety goggles; scissors; and white paper.

Instructions

Note: Before you begin, wash bottle and stopper in warm, soapy water to remove residues. Air-dry, preferably overnight.

Decorating the Cylinder Bottle

1. Mask horizontal bands. Wrap ½in (1.3cm)-wide tape around topmost portion of bottle, overlapping tape at starting point; stretch edge of tape if necessary to hug curved glass. Repeat process to apply parallel bands of tape around bottle one tape width apart. Repeat to tape bottle neck (see illustration A, facing page).

2. Frost horizontal bands. Following manufacturer's instructions and wearing gloves and goggles, apply etching cream to unmasked areas with foam brush. Let cream set 3 to 5 minutes. Wash off cream and remove tape to reveal etched bands (illustration B). Wash glass in soapy water and dry thoroughly.

3. Mask vertical bars. Starting just below neck, affix length of masking tape down side of cylinder. For clean line at top, cut tape with scissors; for easy removal, fold excess tape at bottom back on itself to make tab. Repeat to affix three additional tape lengths, for four bars that divide bottle vertically into quadrants. Increase width of these bars by adding new tape; overlap long edges until unmasked space between bars is reduced to about ½in (1.3cm) (illustration C). Note: If bottle circumference is small, you may not need additional tape.

4. Leaf vertical bars. Using #4 brush, apply thin coat of size to unmasked areas. For clean line, run brush alongside tape edge; try not to brush over it. Apply size to collar and lower portion of bottle neck. Remove tape. Using butter knife, transfer sheet of aluminum leaf to white paper. Tear leaf into postage-stamp size pieces. When size reaches proper tack (10 to 15 minutes), transfer pieces of leaf to sized areas using fingertip, then tamp down with brush (illustration D). Let dry 1 hour, then buff gently with cotton ball. To seal and protect leafed sections, brush on thin coat of clear glaze; do not seal frosted or clear areas. Let dry at least 1 hour.

5. Paint gold accents. Affix two lengths ¼in (6.4mm)

masking tape ⅛in (3.2mm) apart down center of each open vertical section. Make a series of thin, angled lines by applying plaid glass paint directly from dispenser to unmasked area (illustration E). Remove tape immediately after painting to reveal final plaid design (illustration F).

Decorating the Ovoid Bottle

1. Mask circles. Press ⁵/₁₆in (7.9mm) self-adhesive paper dots on bottle surface, randomly spaced about 1in (2.5cm) apart (illustration G).

2. Frost bottle. Refer to Cylinder Bottle, step 2. Frost entire bottle up to neck flange. Remove dots during washing (illustration H).

3. Leaf bottle flange. Refer to Cylinder Bottle, step 4. Brush size onto entire flange. Substitute gold composition leaf for aluminum leaf (illustration I).

4. Add cabochons and gold accents. Squeeze small dot of glue onto one clear circle. Pick up opaline cabochon with tweezers, set into glue and press down gently with cotton swab. Repeat process for remaining circles. Apply gold glass paint directly from dispenser to make circle of small dots around each bead (illustration J), then let dry 15 minutes.

Making the Cylinder Bottle

    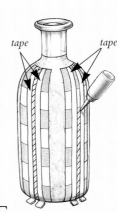 

A. Use tape to mask off horizontal bands.

B. Frost the unmasked areas using etching cream.

C. Adhere the tape vertically to make four wide bars.

D. Apply leaf to the narrow unmasked areas.

E. Add paint between two bands of narrow tape.

F. Peel off the tape promptly after painting.

Decorating the Ovoid Bottle

G. Apply self-stick circles to the bottle at random.

H. Frost the bottle with etching cream to create clear circles.

I. Decorate the flange with gold leaf.

J. Glue a cabachon to each clear circle, then add small dots of paint.

Fabric-Covered Desk Screen

Assembling this two-fold desk screen is very simple: Cover six panels of artist's canvas with fabric, then connect the panels with grosgrain ribbon hinges. Finish by sandwiching the panels together and adding a few decorative touches, such as edge trims, a miniature dollhouse porch railing along the top, and balled feet on the bottom. The desk screen can be used to hide a stack of papers, partition a kitchen countertop, or create a backdrop for a sideboard.

—

This screen was designed with a traditional color scheme: burgundy and gold. For a less formal screen, substitute a country print fabric and paint the railing white.

MATERIALS

- **1yd (.91m) 45in (114.3cm) wide burgundy and gold patterned fabric**
- **1⅝yd (1.5m) ½in (12.7mm) burgundy braided trim**
- **1½yd (1.4m) ¼in (6.4mm) diameter gold cord**
- **¾yd (.7m) 1in (2.5cm) wide burgundy grosgrain ribbon**
- **½yd (.5m) 1in (2.5cm) wide gold grosgrain ribbon**
- **25in (63.5cm) unfinished wooden dollhouse porch railing**
- **Four 1in (2.5cm) diameter unfinished wooden beads**
- **Six 8 x 16in (20.3 x 40.6cm) cardboard-backed artist's canvases**
- **½oz tube (14.8ml) gold paste**
- **16-gauge stainless steel wire**
- **Quick-drying white tacky glue**
- **Spray adhesive**
- **Fray preventive**

YOU'LL ALSO NEED:

hot-glue gun; 1in (2.5cm) paintbrush; small handsaw; 220-grit sandpaper; rotary cutter; scissors; ruler; newsprint; heavy books; pencil; and wire cutters.

Instructions

Covering the Artist's Canvas

1. Adhere fabric to panels. Using rotary cutter, cut six 10 x 18in (25.4 x 45.7cm) fabric rectangles, with 18in (45.7cm) edge running lengthwise along fabric. Working outdoors or in well-ventilated space, lay fabric rectangles right side down on top of several layers of newsprint. Apply spray adhesive following manufacturer's recommendations. Center each artist's panel with canvas side down on fabric and press lightly to adhere. Using scissors, trim away fabric corners in gentle arc about ⅜in (9.5mm) beyond panel corner (see illustration A, facing page).

2. Finish panel edges. Turn each panel over and smooth fabric with palm, then turn panels fabric side down again. Fold each arc-shaped edge onto panel corner, then fold remaining allowances onto back of panel and press to adhere (illustration B).

Assembling the Screen

1. Attach horizontal hinges. Position three panels face down with long edges about ⅜in (9.5mm) apart (illustration C). Cut gold grosgrain ribbon into four 4½in (11.4cm) lengths. Position each ribbon across two panels, 2in (5.1cm) from, and

---

DESIGNER'S TIP

To use the screen as a bulletin board, affix the fabric with two-sided tape instead of spray adhesive. Lay the panels on the untreated fabric (see illustration A, facing page). Apply two-sided tape along the perimeter of the panel, then press the excess fabric onto it (illustration B). Because the front panel fabric is not glued, you'll be able to pin notes and photos to it.

Assembling the Screen

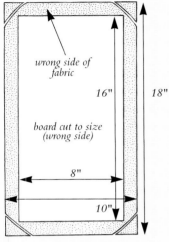

A. **Apply spray adhesive to the fabric, then center each panel, canvas side down, on the fabric. Trim away the fabric corners.**

wrong side of fabric

16"   18"

board cut to size (wrong side)

8"

10"

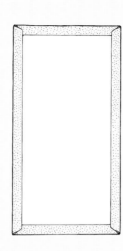

B. **Fold each arc-shaped edge onto the corner, then fold and glue the remaining edges onto the back of the panel.**

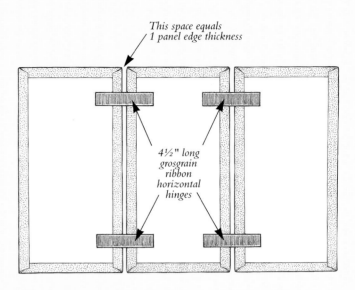

This space equals 1 panel edge thickness

4½" long grosgrain ribbon horizontal hinges

C. **To assemble the screen, position the panels face down, then glue lengths of gold grosgrain ribbon across adjacent panels.**

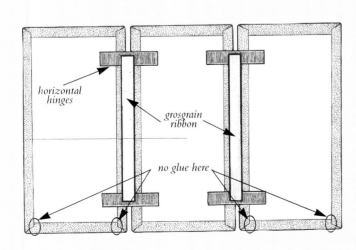

horizontal hinges

grosgrain ribbon

no glue here

D. **Join the two panels along the vertical edges using burgundy ribbon.**

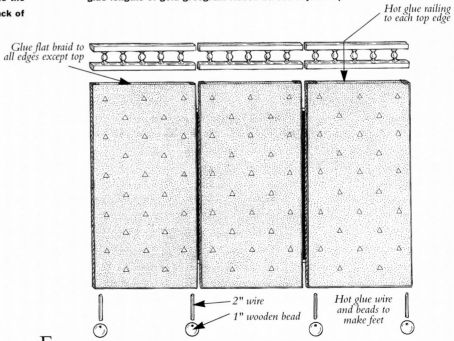

Hot glue railing to each top edge

Glue flat braid to all edges except top

2" wire

1" wooden bead

Hot glue wire and beads to make feet

E. **After gluing the front and back panels together. Then attach the railing to the top of the screen using hot glue, the ball feet to the outside panels, and the narrow gold trim around the base of the railing.**

113

parallel to shorter edges as shown in illustration C. Glue ribbons in place using tacky glue.

2. Attach vertical hinges. Cut burgundy grosgrain ribbon into two 12½in (31.8cm) lengths. Brush tacky glue onto panel edges between horizontal hinges. Press ribbon into place so it joins two panels. Fold raw ends under, exposing ¼in (6.4mm) of horizontal hinge, then glue in place (illustration D).

3. Join front and back panels. Squeeze tacky glue evenly across wrong side of remaining panels, leaving small areas free of glue to wire on feet as shown in illustration D. Position panels glue side down on top of hinged panels and press to adhere.

DESIGNER'S TIP

The screen pictured above will not fold flat because of the choice of wooden dollhouse railing, which is wider than the screen panel thickness, and ball feet made from wooden beads. You can make a screen that folds, however, with a few modifications. Start by making the spacing between the panels equal to two panel thicknesses instead of one. Omit the dollhouse railing and the ball feet and instead glue the flat braid around all of the outer edges.

Weight with heavy books and let dry at least 1 hour, but preferably overnight.

4. Cut and gild railing. Measure and mark dollhouse railing into three 7½–8in (19.1–20.3cm) long identical sections, with marks falling between balusters. Saw along marked lines, then sand lightly. Gild railings and wooden bead feet using gold paste following manufacturer's recommendations.

5. Attach railing and braided trim. Stand screen upright. Run bead of hot glue along top edge of one double panel (illustration E). Set railing section, upside down, into glue, then let set 5–10 seconds. Repeat to attach two remaining railings. Stand screen upside down so railings rest on work surface. Using white tacky glue, attach ½in (12.7mm) braided trim to outer side and bottom edges of each outer panel as well as bottom edge of center panel. Trim ends to fit using scissors, then seal ends with fray preventive.

6. Attach ball feet. Cut four 2in (5.1cm) lengths of steel wire. Insert wires into two outside panels about ¾in (19.1mm) from corner, pushing each wire down through braided trim and in between panel boards to depth of about 1in (2.5cm) (illustration E). Apply hot glue to bead holes, set each bead on wire, and let set 5–10 seconds. Stand screen upright. Use white tacky glue to attach narrow gold cord to each panel around base of railing. Trim to fit, and seal ends with fray preventive. Let screen dry 1 hour.

appendix

Patterns

Handmade Paper Frame (page 62)
Enlarge patterns 200%.

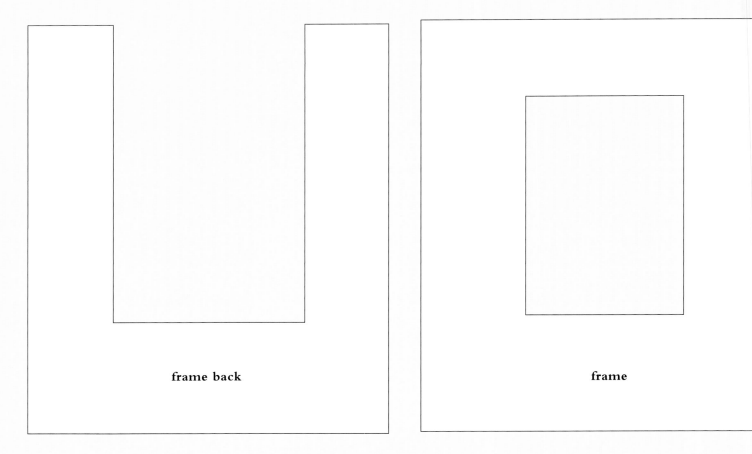

frame back

frame

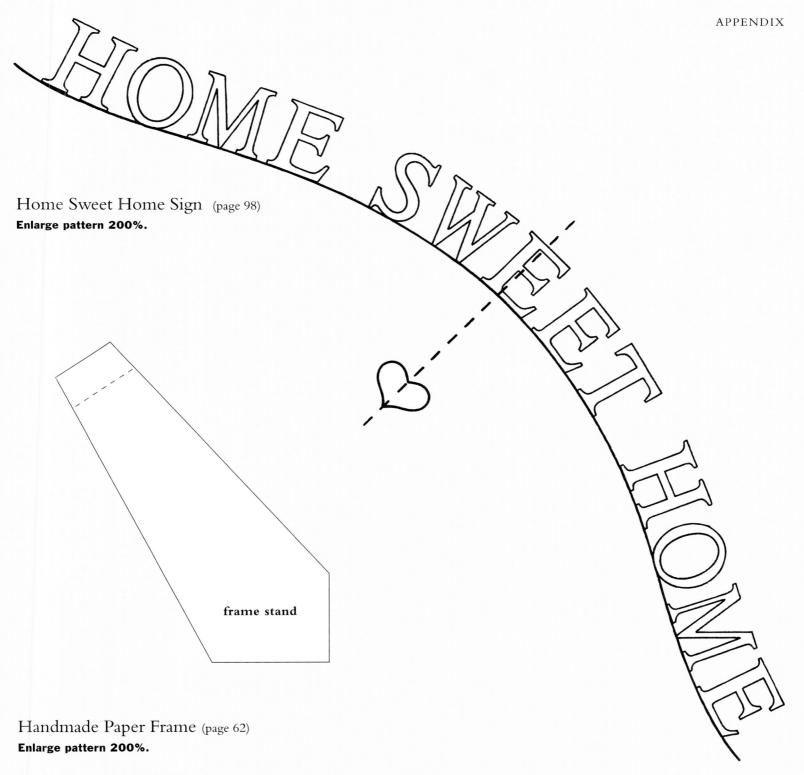

Home Sweet Home Sign (page 98)
Enlarge pattern 200%.

frame stand

Handmade Paper Frame (page 62)
Enlarge pattern 200%.

Sources

Contact each firm individually for an updated price list or catalog.

Art Supplies

Art Supply Warehouse Express
5325 Departure Drive
Raleigh, NC 27604
800-995-6778

Daniel Smith
4150 First Avenue South
P.O. Box 84268
Seattle, WA 98124-5568
800-426-6740

Fidelity Graphic Arts
5601 International Parkway, P.O. Box 155
Minneapolis, MN 55440-0155
800-326-7555

Flax Art and Design
240 Valley Drive
Brisbane, CA 94005
800-547-7778

Graphik Dimensions Ltd.
2103 Brentwood Street
High Point, NC 27263
800-221-0262

Ott's Discount Art Supply
102 Hungate Drive
Greenville, NC 27858
800-356-3289

Pierce Tools
1610 Parkdale Drive
Grants Pass, OR 97527
541-476-1778

Texas Art Supply
2001 Montrose Boulevard
Houston, TX 77006-1299
800-888-9278

Torrington Brush Works
63 Avenue "A", P.O. Box 56
Torrington, CT 06790
800-262-7874 (CT) or **800-525-1416** (FL)

Candle Making

Walnut Hill
Green Lane and Wilson Avenue
P.O. Box 599, Bristol, PA 19007
215-785-6511

General Craft Supplies

American Art Clay Company, Inc.
4717 West 16th Street
Indianapolis, IN 46222
800-374-1600

Circlecraft Supply
P.O. Box 3000
Dover, FL 33527-3000
813-659-0992

Craft Catalog
P.O. Box 1069
Reynoldsburg, OH 43068
800-777-1442

Handcraft Variety Source Book
National Artcraft Company
7996 Darrow Road, Twinsburg, OH 44087
800-793-0152

Lark Books
50 College Street
Asheville, NC 28801-2896
800-284-3388

Maplewood Crafts
Humboldt Industrial Park, 1 Maplewood Dr.
Hazleton, PA 18201-0676
800-899-0134

**Parrish's Cake Decorating Supplies/
Magic Line**
225 West 146th Street
Gardena, CA 90248
310-324-2253 or **800-736-8443**

S&S Worldwide
P.O. Box 515, 75 Mill Street
Colchester, MA 06415-0513
800-243-9232

Vanguard Crafts
P.O. Box 340170, 1081 East 48th Street
Brooklyn, NY 11234
800-662-7238

Painting, Faux Finishing, and Stencils

Artex Manufacturing Company
5894 Blackwelder Street
Culver City, CA 90232-7304
213-870-6000

Artist's Club
13118 NE 4th Avenue
Vancouver, WA 98684
800-845-6507

Cutbill & Company Ltd.
#207-274 Sherman Ave. North
Hamilton, Ontario, Canada L8L 6N6
905-547-8525

The Old Fashioned Milk Paint Co., Inc.
436 Main Street, P.O. Box 222
Groton, MA 01450
508-448-6336

Stu-Art
2045 Grand Avenue
Baldwin, NY 11510
800-645-2855

Stulb's Old Village Paint
P.O. Box 1030
Fort Washington, PA 19034
800-498-7687

Paper Arts
Gold's Artworks Inc.
2100 North Pine Street
Lumberton, NC 28358
800-356-2306

Loose Ends
P.O. Box 20310
Keizer, OR 97307
503-390-7457

Lotus Design
P.O. Box 1993, Union City, CA 94587
800-487-5479

Sewing and Fiber Arts
The Fabric Center
P.O. Box 8212, 485 Electric Avenue
Fitchburg, MA 01420-8212
508-343-4402

Zimman's
76-88 Market Street
Lynn, MA 01901
617-598-9432

Specialty Craft Supplies
Adventures In Crafts
P.O. Box 6058, Yorkville Station
New York, NY 10128
212-410-9793

The Lamp Shop
P.O. Box 3606
Concord, NH 03302-3603
603-224-1603

Lavender Lane
7337 #1 Roseville Road
Sacramento, CA 95842
916-334-4400

Mainely Shades
100 Gray Road
Falmouth, ME 04105
800-624-6359

Canadian Sources
The Cotton Patch
1717 Bedford Hwy
Bedford, NS B4W 1X3
902-861-2782

Bouclair
3149 Sources Bd.
Dollard-des-Ormeaux, QC
514-683-4711

La Maison de Calico
324 Lakeshore Blvd
Pointe Claire, QC H9S 4L7
514-695-0728

Omer DeSerres
334 Ste.-Catherine East
Montreal, QC H2X 1l7
800-363-0318 or **514-842-6637**

Rockland Textiles
2487 Kaladar Avenue
Ottawa, ON K1V 8B9
613-526-0333

Bouclair
1233 Donald Street
Ottawa, ON K1J 8W3
613-744-3982

Designer Fabric Outlet
1360 Queen St. W
Toronto, ON M6K 1L7
416-531-2810

The Fabric Cottage
16 Crowfoot Terrace NW
Calgary, AB T3G 4J8
403-241-3070

The Quilting Bee
1026 St. Mary's Rd
Winnipeg, MB R2M 3S6
204-254-7870

Homespun Craft Emporium
250A 2nd Avenue S
Saskatoon, SK S7K 1K9
306-652-3585

The Cloth Shop
4415 West 10th Avenue
Vancouver, BC V6R 2H8
604-224-1325

Metric Conversions

ENGLISH EQUIVALENTS

¼₄in = .4mm

⅓₂in = .8mm

⅓₅in = 1mm

¹⁄₁₆in = 1.6mm

⅛in = 3.2mm

¼in = 6.4mm

⅜in = 9.5mm or .9cm

½in = 12.7mm or 1.3cm

⅝in = 15.9mm or 1.6cm

¾in = 19.1mm or 1.9cm

⅞in = 22.2mm or 2.2cm

1in = 2.5cm

2in = 5.1cm

3in = 7.6cm

4in = 10.2cm

5in = 12.7cm

6in = 15.2cm

7in = 17.8cm

8in = 20.3cm

9in = 22.9cm

10in = 25.4cm

1 qt = .95L

1 pint = .47L

½ cup = 118ml

1 cup = .24L

3 lb = 1.36kg

1 fluid oz = 29.6ml

English System to Metric

TO CHANGE:	INTO:	MULTIPLY BY:
Inches	Millimeters	25.400
Inches	Centimeters	2.540
Feet	Meters	.305
Yards	Meters	.914
Pints	Liters	.473
Quarts	Liters	.946
Gallons	Liters	3.780
Ounces	Grams	28.400
Pounds	Kilograms	.454

Metric to English System

TO CHANGE:	INTO:	MULTIPLY BY:
Millimeters	Inches	.039
Centimeters	Inches	.394
Meters	Feet	.280
Meters	Yards	1.090
Liters	Pints	2.110
Liters	Quarts	1.060
Liters	Gallons	.264
Grams	Ounces	.035

Acknowledgments

A collection of this scope requires the talents of many people. Generous thanks to those at *Handcraft Illustrated* who assisted in its preparation: for their creative and technological acumen, Senior Editor Michio Ryan and Directions Editor Candie Frankel; for manifesting the spirit and aesthetic attributes of each project, Art Director Amy Klee, Photographer Carl Tremblay, and Stylist Ritch Holben; for intelligent and seamless project management and manuscript magic, Executive Editor Barbara Bourassa; and finally, to Christopher Kimball, publisher of *Handcraft Illustrated*, whose original vision informed the work on all levels. Thanks also to Angela Miller and Coleen O'Shea, of The Miller Agency, who believed in the project and gathered this creative team in an extraordinarily fulfilling process.

About Handcraft Illustrated

Handcraft Illustrated is a sophisticated, yet accessible how-to magazine featuring craft and home decorating projects. Each 52-page quarterly issue includes approximately 35 different projects. The projects are accompanied by a full-color photograph, a complete materials list, precise step-by-step directions, and concise hand-drawn illustrations. All projects featured in the magazine are fully tested to ensure that the readers can make the designer-quality craft projects at home.

Special departments include Quick Tips, an ongoing series of professional craft secrets, shortcuts, and techniques; Notes from Readers, providing detailed answers to readers' problems; Quick Home Accents, a unique pairing of materials and accessories designed to spur creative craft or decorating solutions; The Perfect Gift, offering creative solutions for designing, making, and packaging your own unique gifts; Quick Projects, a series of "theme-and-variation" projects featuring 4 to 6 versions of one easy-to-make craft; and Sources and Resources, a retail and mail-order directory for locating materials and supplies used in the issue.

For a free trial issue of *Handcraft Illustrated*, call 800-933-4447.

Credits

All color photography: Carl Tremblay, except as noted.

Containers

12 French Tinware Cachepot
Illustration: Michelle Armatrula Styling: Ritch Holben

18 Arts and Crafts–Style Bandbox
Illustration: Mary Newell DePalma Styling: Ritch Holben

22 Star Frost Vase
Illustration: Nenad Jakesevic Styling: Ritch Holben

26 Painted Plaid Cachepot
Illustration: Nenad Jakesevic Styling: Ritch Holben

Lighting

32 Laminated Leaf Lampshade
Illustration: Nenad Jakesevic

36 Red Velvet Candleshade
Illustration: Michael Gellatly (A-E) and Nenad Jakesevic (F-H)
Styling: Ritch Holben

40 Fabric-Covered Lampshade
Illustration: Judy Love (dia.1 & 2) and Nenad Jakesevic (A-F)

46 Seashell Candles
Illustration: Nenad Jakesevic Styling: Ritch Holben

Frames

52 Vintage Wallpaper Frame
Illustration: Michael Gellatly

56 Antique Brass Frames
Illustration: Nenad Jakesevic Styling: Ritch Holben

60 Handmade Paper Frame
Illustration: Judy Love Patterns: Roberta Frauwirth

64 Rose Petal Frame
Color photography: Stephen Mays Illustration: Wendy Wray
Styling: Sylvia Lachter

Furniture

70 Faux Marble Tabletop
Illustration: Mary Newell DePalma (A & C),
Nenad Jakesevic (B)
Styling: Gabrielle Derrick de Papp/Team

74 Farmhouse Table
Color samples: Vi and Stu Cutbill

78 English Manor Ottoman
Illustration: Mary Newell DePalma
Styling: Gabrielle Derrick de Papp/Team

84 Country Stripe Cupboard
Illustration: Nenad Jakesevic Styling: Ritch Holben

Decorative Items

90 Classic Carriage Clock
Illustration: Mary Newell DePalma

96 Home Sweet Home Sign
Illustration: Mary Newell DePalma
Styling: Ritch Holben Patterns: Roberta Frauwirth

100 Faux Limoges Hinged Boxes
Illustration: Mary Newell DePalma Styling: Ritch Holben

106 Frosted Perfume Bottles
Illustration: Michael Gellatly
Styling: Ritch Holben

110 Fabric-Covered Desk Screen
Illustration: Mary Newell DePalma
Styling: Gabrielle Derrick de Papp/Team

Index